MW00789872

"Views from Jackass Hill offers wonderful tapestry of western life."

–Bea Romer, former first lady of Colorado, and staunch proponent of literary and early childhood reading.

"Three Ladies of Letters, applying their love of literature, give us glimpses into the magic and mundane, the causes and courses, the humor and heartaches which make them the deep and interesting people they are today. We have known these ladies for years (and many like them) and now know much more what's behind the smiles. This is truly a joy to read!"

–John R. Phillips, Attorney at Law and Chairman of the South Metro Arts Organization (CO).

"While reading Views from Jackass Hill, I couldn't help but think of a crazy quilt. The thoughts, musings and tales from different women are all mixed together in a fascinating whole. You have to be a little bit wild and crazy to put your heart out there like these three women have done. Hats off to them all!"

–Mary Chrisman, Reiki Master, Fiber Artist, and Visionary.

"This book is a potpourri of stories, poems, and limericks from a group of wickedly talented writers. Immensely entertaining, these stories will surely give you a swift kick in the tail!"

–Erik Highland, Author, Filmmaker, Literate.

Views from Jackass Hill..."A witty and wise compilation of poetry and prose from three of the area's finest."*

–Lou Malandra, Actor, Poet, Professor

VIEWS...
From JACKASS HILL

AN ECLECTIC LITERARY COLLECTION

Enjoy!
Claire Leraan Brown

De gustibus non est disputandum

Jeanne Freed

Shirley Meier

CLAIRE LERAAN BROWN,
JEANNE FREED, SHIRLEY MEIER

Wasteland Press

Louisville, KY USA
www.wastelandpress.com

Views From Jackass Hill
An Eclectic Literary Collection
by Claire Leraan Brown,
Jeanne Freed, Shirley Meier

Second Printing – September, 2004
Cover design by Bob Taylor
Illustrations by Shirley Meier

ISBN: 1-932852-57-3

Printed in the U.S.A.

JACKASS HILL WRITERS' GROUP

(So what's in a name?)

To the amusement of all who see it, there really is a Jackass Hill in Littleton, Colorado, with a view and street sign. In the early twentieth century, the hill was used as grazing land for burros, destined for use by the military as pack animals in World War I. When the animals were not requisitioned, the owner set them free.

Because our writer's group meets near Jackass Hill and most of our members live in the vicinity, the name seemed a natural fit. We considered changing it to something more sophisticated, but decided we weren't.

In the spirit of our Jackass namesakes, we have been spurred on by their example. With hard work, a stubborn determination and a bit of an attitude, we offer a collection of short stories, essays, limericks, and poems. Our works emanate from diverse influences, including personal experiences, survival against the odds, and "free for all" musings.

Through a bond of creative friendship, three of us from our group contributed to this book. Lively debates aside, we have agreed to take no responsibility for each other's work.

This volume is dedicated to those perceptive and intuitive readers who realize there is a bit of the jackass in each of us. Enjoy our Views from Jackass Hill!

Claire Leraan Brown
Jeanne Freed
Shirley Meier

TABLE OF CONTENTS

MULEHEADED

ANIMAL

Donkey, mule, Jackass
Laden, lean, sure-footed friend
–Man's mean verbal curse.

Shirley Meier

GUTTER LUST*

Jeanne Freed

Winter's freeze and thaw temperatures created glacial deposits surrounding our home worthy of an attempt by Sir Edmund Hillary. New gutters, though necessary, were an expense that less than thrilled me. This was one of those homeowner upgrades that I'd never be able to show off to my friends.

A well referenced installer arrived with samples, extolling the benefits of seamless galvanized steel gutters. I wasn't impressed, but my husband suddenly had a gleam in his eye.

"They're five inches wide!" he praised.

"That's nice," I responded.

"He rolls them seamless with a steel bender, right out in front of the house! Wait `til you see it!"

"Can't wait," I managed to say, thoroughly dumbfounded by his excitement.

"He'll solder the seams with a propane torch. These babies are gonna be lifetime." That news I kinda liked, but I said nothing.

So, the gutter man installed the new gutters and they worked. He showed me how they dispatched water to the proper locations, but I still remained less than fascinated. In my mind, I only saw my great gift ideas turn into lengths of bent metal.

My husband could hardly wait to inspect the new gutters. "These are fantastic, look at the craftsmanship." His fingers ran reverently across the span of the front porch

"Uh huh," I said slowly. "But I think we should paint them to match the trim."

My husband looked at me somewhat indulgently. "We will. But with steel, you have to wait until it seasons and loses the burnish."

"Oh." I replied, because I know this means he has no intention of painting anything during football season.

The very next day, the doorbell rang, and standing on the doorstep was a male neighbor. "I see you got new gutters, mind if I take a look?"

"Look all you want," I said Feeling I should contribute to the experience, I wandered around the house with him.

"These are very nice." His hand crept up and touched a gutter on a low overhang. Desire appeared in his eyes and his fingers fondled bent edges. He left armed with the phone number of the installer and furtive backward glances aimed at the gutters, of course.

3

The next morning, a man I vaguely knew showed up at our schoolbus stop with his kids in tow. He marched right up to me and said, "I hear you got new gutters." Somewhat surprised by the speed of the grapevine, I nodded dumbly.

"Can I see them?"

Once again I led a tour. He seemed to be very attracted to my downspouts, and couldn't help but caress my end caps. "I just love my new gutters," I gushed.

"I can see why," he sighed in admiration.

I knew the horrible truth. My most attractive feature is my seamless galvanized all steel gutters. For weeks, cars slowed as they passed, and more men seemed to be walking their dogs. I heard the tapping of gutter installation throughout the neighborhood.

Our gutters are still hanging and doing their main job, seasoning and burnishing. They may get painted after the holiday season, or football season. Or was that baseball... or maybe fishing?

*GUTTER LUST first appeared in ALASKA MAGAZINE/Best Humor 1998

LET'S DO FLOWERS FOR LUNCH...?*

Claire L. Brown

Invited to attend a fine luncheon,
I accepted within a few hours,
When, alas, I heard through the grapevine
The menu included wild flowers.

I'm fond of being adventurous
And like trying many things new,
But flowers to abate my appetite?
Should I? Well, would you?

I imagined sampling cinquefoil,
And finding nasturtiums elite.
Can it be that petunias and asters
Are included in items to eat?

Might they concoct a columbine sandwich
For a morsel described as incredible?
Or indulge in mint and rose petal pate'
Which sounds both inane and inedible?

If sweet n'sour iris
Should happen to be their passion,
Some guests may claim they're peculiar,
Yet others insist they're in fashion.

Should I munch on bitter marigolds
Or other plants equally awful?
Methinks I'll protest these so called treats,
Suggesting they may be unlawful.

It's true that Socrates ate hemlock,
Which led to his rapid demise.
When selecting a flower for nibbling,
His fate is `a word to the wise.'

Exotic blossoms for summer dining
May put smiles on some people's faces,
But when I pick garden posies,
I'd sooner put them in vases.

LET'S DO FLOWERS FOR LUNCH...? won the Littleton, Colorado, KOEBEL LIBRARY POETRY CONTEST in May, 2001.

OUT TO PASTURE*
Shirley Meier

"Come on now, you old plugs," I shouted and smiled, lightly snapping the reins over the broad glistening backs of Roy and Diamond, the sturdy work horses who were also my trusted companions. On that warm languid day, I remember them pulling on the harnesses with steady motion, their glossy chestnut bodies moving in the rhythm of their task.

High on the hay rake's metal seat, I sat perched behind them, a proud twelve year old girl with pig tails sticking out of my straw hat, helping with the family's ranching chores. We were working a patch of newly mown grass and alfalfa, with rows and rows of drying hay lying in wide contours across the land. My father said that it was about time to put the horses "out to pasture" but that I could still use the team this summer. Although most of the ranch work was done by machinery, I was glad that Roy and Diamond had these days in the field and I had a chance to do grown up work.

They pulled forward harder in their traces because of my not so subtle encouragement but they soon fell back into their usual gait. I didn't really mind. We'd finished most of the field already. The steady slow pace of the old animals allowed me time for youthful daydreaming so I let the reins hang loose with only an occasional reminder. They knew the way, having done it for years, but they wheezed and stumbled once in a while. Little did I realize that they could still run like three year olds.

The rake was constructed in a tee formation with the wooden pole, or tongue, extending forward between the horses whose harnesses hooked up to it. The span of the awkward implement's frame extended far out to both sides where it was attached to high spoke wheels. Half circular steel teeth humped over the back of the frame to catch and roll the grass and they reminded me of an old fashioned lady's bustle.

Getting near the end of the field, I released the lever that controlled the raising of the rake's teeth. This maneuver required that I edge forward in the seat in order to push down hard with my extended right foot. I was strong for my age, but my legs still didn't quite reach the adult span that was required. However, it was the only real challenge of the job.

Far down at the other end of the field, almost half a mile away, my brother scooped up the dried rows with the fork lift. Mounted on the

7

front of the tractor, it looked like a giant praying mantis out on a foraging venture. With the fork filled, he drove to the stack where my father waited. After the hay was dumped on top, Father rearranged it and stomped it into place while my brother went for more. Every hour or so they rotated their jobs for a break in routine and exertion.

Looking at the distant stacks, I realized how much they looked like my mother's bread loaves, newly baked and browned, sitting in a row on the counter. When finished, the hay loaves received oval tops too, which allowed the water to run off. Their crusty mahogany color developed after the weather aged them. That ruddy brown hue also attached itself to the soil and the scoria, a broken rock that was used on local North Dakota roads. It was reflected in late sunsets, the coat of the horses, and even my own auburn hair contained a reddish hint.

Up and down, back and forth across the field we went. The routine hadn't become monotonous yet on this, my second day out. Diamond snorted. I wiped my forehead, lifting the tip of the hat, but the moderating prairie breeze helped the July afternoon from becoming oppressive.

The fence to the pasture ran directly beside the alfalfa field. Both were bordered with the highway leading to town. Every once in a while, I spotted a pickup truck coming down a graveled road way up on the side of the hills. It sent a dust trail to the sky before hitting the paved stretch. Sometimes a driver, traveling along the highway, would honk at me and I'd wave. I wondered if they noticed I was a girl.

Earlier the train of long freight cars, bound for Montana, went by on the distant tracks. The sound of the sharp whistle as it neared the crossing and the clicking of its wheels carried through the valley, causing even the horses to notice. But now all was still except for their puffing and the stinging, thin swing of their tails whisking flies. I hummed contentedly, looking at the deep blue sky where a few puffy clouds hung closes to the western horizon. In the early morning when we started, many birds had flitted in and around the grass, but now it was deserted, except for the slow circling of a hawk overhead. He'd been there a long time, waiting for a careless mouse or gopher, disturbed by the passing rake, to dart from cover.

Father had reminded me to watch out for snakes when he gave me a stern lecture about being careful with horses. They might get spooked if they slithered in front of them. So far, I hadn't seen any, even though spotting a rattle this time of year wasn't unusual. It didn't scare me, because I was far off the ground. They'd simply get rolled into the hay cylinder and dumped, probably no worse for the wear. I did look out especially for rabbit and prairie dog holes because I didn't want one of my favorite horses to break a leg. Also the narrow rake's wheels could get twisted in them.

We went back and forth, getting closer to the pasture and were almost done with the cut section. My eyes wandered beyond the fence to the creek, or as we all called it, the crick. Sluggish or often dry in mid summer, it was adorned with the rare jewels of the vast plains trees. Not just some scrub brush but actual decent elms, cedars, box elders, poplars, and a sprinkling of wild fruit bushes.

That creek provided my childhood with a haven of play and pretend. Sometimes I rode Diamond there to get the cows but mostly I wandered with the dogs in imaginative adventures. My brother and I had played cowboys and Indians on its banks where the actual characters had once lived. I liked playing hide and seek but since my brother was much older, it took a lot of cunning to fool him. However, I knew good hiding places in the cottonwoods' hollow trunks and the wash outs left from the spring's runoff.

I glanced down the valley toward the far distant town where only my school's belfry, the church steeples and grain elevators rose clearly above the rolling fields and prairie. Even though stirrings of far away places sometimes fluttered in me at night when I heard the far off train, the nearby scene still held my young allegiance. Serene summer days of picking choke cherries and gathering wild flowers shimmered like a western mirage in my mind and my heart.

The filled rake interrupted my dreamy interlude. I stretched and released the lever. My muscles hurt a bit, I realized. Because the seat didn't have a back, I was getting rather limp but I consoled myself because we were almost done. Then I could take a break. We always brought water and a little snack in a metal lunch bucket that we stashed in the shade of the hay stacks. Perhaps Father would even bestow a few glowing remarks about my excellent performance on the job. He often turned his sweaty sunburned face to the sky and breeze and exclaimed how much he liked this life. It flowed easily from yesterday into tomorrow, I also thought.

Later, I'd go over to the sand hills behind the ranch on the south side. Raking there wouldn't take long, because even in good years like this one was, not much grew on their shinning slopes The cut hay, caught by the rake's teeth, rotated, turned and twisted into rolls like fluffy fiber crepes. With a soft plop, they fell to the stubble ground. I took pride in the long line, knowing how important winter feed for the stock was.

With another push, I lowered the rattling steel prongs while the steady gentle gait of the horses continued forward. The sweet smell of the tossed hay coupled with the cadence of the horses proved hypnotic as we went up and down, across and around, getting closer to the end of the row. I turned the horses into the last row next to the fence along the pasture.

CRAAAAACCK!

It sounded like a pistol shot or clap of crisp thunder but it actually was the wheel's axle hitting a fence post dead on. The sound echoed along the old timber frame of the rake, vibrating from the force of the impact. I had been careless and swung too wide. Startled, the horses bolted forward with a snap of the jingling harnesses. The wheezing frightened alarm of their nostrils pierced the air as the reins flew up and out of my hands. With the jolt, I was catapulted forward into the air, hat flying of.Falling forward, I landed on the rake's pole broadside and hit my nose hard.

Instinctively I hooked on to it with a giant quick grab; the horses' churning hoofs were on each side of my face. My legs mysteriously and miraculously wound around the pole just like a monkey clutching a moving branch. I knew if I fell, the deadly prongs would puncture my flailing body and roll me into a bloody lifeless sausage.

The pole bobbed erratically and the horses bounded away. I lost balance and swung around the pole, hanging on with frightened tenacity. Somehow the momentum carried me again to the top. My days on the school's climbing bars may have prepared me for this but now there was no solid ground below. The stubble line raced by me in dizzy curving lines. Craning my neck, I tried looking toward the frame but the dangerous swaying prevented me from edging back to it.

Roy's hooves flew perilously close to me, kicking up the dirt, catching my hair and pulling my head over, but I clung to the pole with manic strength. I heard the fire alarm whinny of Diamond who was the gentlest of horses rise above the hissing of the rake's steel teeth as they clanged against each other. Through my dusty eye lashes, I saw the rake with the menacing swords aimed at me, catching the hay and debris, turning everything over and over with increased chaos.

The horses ran wild, panicked now by loss of control, crisscrossing the rows, jarring the rake so much that it flew off the ground on one side, coming down with a bang. Then it was thrown up again. The teeth, turned to daggers, gouged into the earth as the rake crashed and hit. Several broke off by the force, sending shinning pieces spinning through the air in all directions. One hit Roy who gave out a piercing scream as he plunged forward.

I hung on. I was dizzy, my muscles cramping. The pole's tongue jarred up and down with staccato speed and from below, the sharp spears aimed at me, rattling like sinister snakes. Roy and Diamonds' powerful legs churned beside me. There was no way to release the lever and bring up the teeth off the ground. Horrified, I braced myself but my wrists suddenly felt like tiny threads holding numbed fingers. My legs slipped off, hitting the ground where they were tossed and flipped around like a limp rag doll's limbs. My mouth was choking with dirt and I closed my eyes in terror. I coughed and screamed. I think I howled a prayer through the melee.

Then I felt a surge of freedom, a soaring instant of not being connected. The horses were flying beside in a brown red cloud and we were all ensconced in this gritty fog, dark with dust. Up and down and forward we went into oblivion. Flying, floating, falling.

The long moment stopped in time.

It was quiet. I opened my eyes and could see the blazing sun. I blinked and jerked my head to the side, blinded by the piercing rays. I felt the dirt heavy and caked on my eyelashes and face. For a split second, I saw the field, the pasture's fence, and the creek beyond. Then everything blurred, the hooves pounded again, the rake jarred me, the teeth hissed. My mind exploded; I saw stars and shooting stars. It was quiet again and I was alive, I knew it. I opened my crusted eyes again to the sun. Taking a deep long breath, I looked up and saw the hawk slowly circling above me.

A stranger's face telescoped into my world. "God, are you all right?" he said.

The man cradled me in his arms. I felt the warmth of his breath and body. I heard the tractor and my father's shouts rising above the sound. The pounding in my head or my heart started as he and my brother reached me.

"What happened? What happened?" Their frantic questions reverberated and echoed through the chambers of my mind.

"I saw the runaway from the road," said the unfamiliar voice. "She fell down like a sack of potatoes when the horses jolted but she hung unto the pole. I could see it. I stopped my truck and started running, so I didn't quite see what else happened."

The men placed me on the fork lift, full of hay, and my father held me as we sped toward the ranch. The padded bounce soothed me as my brother negotiated the tractor across the rippling ruts of the field. I felt my head clear and tasted blood coming from my nose. From my high vantage point on top of the fork lift, I saw the crazed horses bounding ahead of us for the ranch in the distance. Only a splintered portion of the snapped pole bound them together now. Across the ditch I saw the upturned rake.

Mother charged toward us as we got to the ranch, her hysterical voice shouting up at me. She'd obviously seen the runaway horses as they entered the yard in their stampede. I could even see the animals, stomping and unsure at the barn door. When my brother lowered the fork lift, I was carried off by my father.

"I'm O.K. I'm O.K.," I insisted with a fair amount of enthusiasm in my blurry state.

"It doesn't look like she's got any broken bones, not even her nose," Father told Mother after he examined me. Ranchers, far from medical facilities, were experienced at quick diagnosis of animals, fowl and family but my parents' faces showed frightened concern. "She really got knocked around, according to a truck driver who helped us. A real nice guy."

"Let's get you into the house," said my mother, wiping my bloody face with her apron.

"Oh, just let me lean against the barn," I said.

Mother didn't ask what happened because she knew. An accident, a lesson learned the hard way, all their eyes told me. I agreed with them but a creeping guilt made me continue. "I'm so sorry, so sorry. They just got away from me, " I said.

I could see Roy and Diamond prancing around in a tangle of straps and splashed foam covered their nostrils and long faces; their ears lay down and their eyes darted wildly. I knew they wanted to go into their place of refuge and escape me.

Father barked, waving to my brother, "Get those damn horses in the stalls."

When the door opened, the frantic animals dashed to their familiar places inside, like soldiers fleeing to foxholes during battle. Suddenly I also wanted the stability of the big barn but it swayed as I put my bruised hands against the siding. Its safety evaded me as my knees weakened and wobbled. Shock set it and finished the job of the galloping hooves and vibrating teeth.

Long gashes; lots of dark bruises and a sore nose were my only major physical complaints but I was often hot and cold, asleep and waking up to a recurring nightmare. Mother called the doctor for advice but what I needed was rest and recovery. They'd care for me at home. Her blankets and vigilance saw me through the next few days.

Fitfully I thought about the accident. I couldn't remember clearly but I realized that only the abrupt turn of the horses at the same time that I fell could have saved me. Only that and a greater power, I knew. One

12

side of the implement must have flown off the ground, allowing my body to escape below. When I started to feel better, the family asked me questions and speculated. My profound response, which pleased everyone, was that the hawk alone knew the answer as he was the only observer.

A few days later I limped to the fence to see Roy and Diamond grazing in the pasture. I called their names, but in vane. They immediately trotted away.

"Come here, you old plugs," I insisted. "It's me, your buddy."

Roy lifted his head and made a hissing sound. Diamond just lowered his. Yes, they were old and spooked. They'd never work again and I knew then that my only contact with them would be from afar.

"Diamond. Roy," I begged.

Wary of my approach, they moved to the shadows of the trees. Tearfully, I leaned against the fence as part of my childhood receded with them.

*OUT TO PASTURE was a 2004 writing contest winner at SOUTHGLENN (CO) LIBRARY

THE WORLD IS FULL OF GODZILLAS
Claire L. Brown

The world is full of godzillas,
Attilas and Camillas,
Who wink o'er their gin,
Hell bent to win
Castles and flotillas.

At ease with meaningless chatter
On subjects too frivolous to matter.
Plotting and striving,
Endless conniving.
Severed heads served on a platter.

While the citizenry reside in lethargy,
Failing to recall past treachery,
Godzillas can lie
Looking straight in the eye
Amidst self indulgence and lechery.

A Godzilla is truly an anthropoid,
Never to `ape,' but to avoid.
Shan't we bemoan
A chimp on the throne
Of refinement quite devoid?

CLASH OF THE TITANS
Jeanne Freed

Rumors abound that females experiencing their "monthlies" within a household will eventually gravitate toward one another until all concerned are in cycle sync. From my experience, this is a Utopian theory. Knowing its hard enough to keep myself in check, it is nearly impossible to keep my daughters' multiple mood shifts under control. At best, we experience a mere week of consensual calm every month.

My middle schooler gets out of bed ready to wage battle, entirely based on how her hair looks. On puffy hair days she moans, "I'm bloated and chubby... this waistband's too tight... I need new jeans?" Frizzy hair days yield high voltage rants. "I just set my pencil down! Who took it? (Foot stomp) I can't believe you people!" Wavy hair means a sudden stomach ache at bus time and a panicked request for a ride. Compressed ringlets mean she's wound up as tight as a canary with lockjaw. She has equated her hair to a hedgehog's bristles, a dandelion puff, a circus poodle's poofs, a scouring pad's texture, and "Bob's Big Boys" errant flip. There isn't a line of gel, mousse, shampoo, conditioner or frizz control we haven't tried, but she remains biologically regulated by the stuff growing on her head.

My high school senior has perfected the art of stiletto tongue, leaving her victim feeling like a filleted fish. Her tactic is embedded in the belief that attack is the best defense. She loves to preface every comment with implied reference to my failings, such as, "If you could possibly spare me a moment. . ." or " I know you're busy, so don't bother with me". Before I can sputter out the words "You're late", she has already thrown down the gauntlet with, "Real nice, I come home and nobody even says hello."

Fool that I am, I say, "Hello, you're late."

"Yeah, and I suppose you were never late!" she snaps. This move is calculated to make me reflect on my wicked past, while she slips off to her bedroom.

But while the teenagers concentrate on raising their hormonal levels, mine are waging war with menopausal decline. Some days, I can literally feel the roots of my hair begin to smolder. With a warning flash, searing heat envelops my body, and my fingers move automatically to the thermostat, finding comfort while the rest of the family piles on sweaters, seeing their breath in frosty puffs. Still, I'm convinced my power is immense and no one will dare ask, "What's for dinner?" But foolishly they do. My brain is a paragraph ahead of my mouth, ruminating various options. There's the obvious, "Look in the pot on the stove", or perhaps a sarcastic and disgusting answer, "Sea slug flambé with a side of fresh cut kudzu".

Somehow I manage to simply recite the boring menu, just as the time before this and before that. But I also add, "There is no dessert; please clean the kitchen afterward . . . and I'm going to a movie. Love you, bye".

I intend to remain supreme.

Period!

WHERE YA' HEADED?

Claire L. Brown

I met Eddie Vahn in a small nondescript diner off highway #80 somewhere in western Nebraska. Since it was pouring rain with a heavy wind, I decided to pull off the road, have an early lunch, and hope that weather conditions would lighten up in the meantime. Eddie Vahn, coincidentally, had made a similar decision.

We both were eating at the counter to save time, having destinations to reach by nightfall. His giant hands were wrapped around a super burger, making it look hike a child's portion. Expecting him to wolf it down, I was surprised to see him nibble at it like a chipmunk. He seemed preoccupied until suddenly requesting me to pass the ketchup. As I handed it over to him I observed his pale unshaven face, dark bloodshot eyes, and scar across one cheek, making him appear to smirk.

"Where ya' headed,?" he asked with a faint (almost toothless) smile.

I said, "I'm traveling from Colorado to northern Minnesota."

"Oh yeah? Ya' mean you're goin' to the ice box of the nation on purpose?"

I couldn't help but laugh. "I'm going to Duluth, located on Lake Superior, which happens to have short, but beautiful summers."

"Oh , maybe so, but how about them arctic winters,?" he teased. "I grew up mostly around Omaha, and we ain't never seen long polar bear winters like yours."

When I insisted I preferred Duluth's heavy winters over Omaha's hot humid summers, he blurted out with a grin, "You gotta' be kiddin' me!"

When I asked about his family, he narrowed his eyes, lowered his head, and stared blankly for a few awkward seconds.

"I'm sorry," I half whispered. "I didn't mean to pry or upset you. It's none of my business."

"No, no, no," he stammered. "It's just that, ...well, my flea bit' brothers made some damned stupid choices, not jest one, but one after another, 'til they got theirselves in deep trouble. Now one's in a stinkin' jail, and the other's in a funny farm for gambling, drugs, and most any other addiction you can think up. At least I had the sense to take off for California."

Eddie sighed, shook his head, and changed the subject before I could utter a word.

17

Catching the waitress's attention, he said, "Hey, I got me a problem I need new windshield wipers for my ole' Ford truck. Ya' know where I can get any?"

Obligingly, the waitress replied, "You're in luck. There's a place just three blocks down the street that'll have anything you need."

Since it was still raining I offered him a ride to the garage and back. As we stepped outside I noticed his battered old blue Ford truck with California license plates. In spite of the ride, Eddie was drenched by the time his wipers were in place. Since they seemed to work, I waved goodbye.

In parting, he advised, "A nice lady like you shouldn't be offering rides to no strangers. It ain't smart."

I quickly agreed, saying defensively, "I don't usually, and probably won't again. Thanks for the reminder."

A couple of days later a front page headline in a small town newspaper caught my eye: WOMAN MURDERED WHILE HELPING EXCAPEE IN STOLEN TRUCK. The remainder of the column described his battered old blue truck with California plates, confirming my worst fears. It went on to give the grizzly, gruesome details. The woman had been bludgeoned with a tire iron, beheaded, and left in a roadside ditch. I read until my hands were shaking too much to hold the paper.

"He warned me," I gasped. "It could so easily have been me!"

TRAIL DUST

DROUGHT

Shining empty skies
Rabbit Bush, Yucca, Sedum
–High, dry, still smiling.

Shirley Meier

LEGACY*

Shirley Meier

(Written in honor of the 1983 centennial
celebration of Glen Ullin, North Dakota.)

More than a gusty gully but really less than a glen,
The place was named with a swirl of romance and pen
As the surveyor patterned the shallow vale,
Marking lots, acres, quarters   all up for sale.

Emptied, the first natives were gone. Then came the train,
Bringing English, Russians and Germans in the main,
Belching forth smoke and these immigrants en masse
Who stood, stared and staked the undulating grass.

It became home: a crude cradle but firm and deep,
Etched against the endless, huge horizon's sweep,
This settlement near the rolling plains and butte
Was really just a dot on the coast to coast route.

Trees, then houses rose near the slender stream.
Homesteaders fenced and tilled, filling their dream,
With stock grazing, and coyotes howling from afar.
Later came a church, school, store, elevator, and bar.

The land formed and forced the pioneer's tough image
But many of them would be lost, in spite of courage,
To distant denser towns which offered them more.
Through a hundred years of drought, depression, war.

Some would return, with traveled and wiser eyes,
To visit cherished family, friends, but with sighs
Were aware that few of their own children's faces
Would ever be gladdened by those proud prairie places.

*LEGACY first appeared in the BISMARCK (ND) TRIBUNE in 1983.

21

DEAR MOM*

Claire L. Brown

I don't want to remember her this way, I thought, as I watched Mom decline. Alzheimer's disease had stolen my mother, and replaced her with a near stranger, forgetful, repetitive and sometimes belligerent.

Twice a year I flew from Denver to Orlando to spend two weeks visiting her in a health center. She had been moved there from her retirement condominium after becoming confused, and walking two miles down the street in her bedroom slippers. Following the incident, I bought her a silver slip on bracelet with her identification secured on the underside. Presenting it to her as a personal gift rather than an I.D. bracelet, she accepted it graciously.

Late one morning while waiting to take her to lunch at a nearby cafe, she emerged from her bedroom smiling and radiant wearing white gloves and a fancy hat that matched her pale pink evening suit. When I suggested the cafe was casual, she said, "Oh, of course, silly me. I'll change, and only be a minute." She reappeared without hat and gloves, wearing the same evening suit with dark green knee highs and white tennis shoes.

"Off we go then," was all I could say. During lunch Mom expressed delight at the pleasant new restaurant I had found, oblivious to the fact that we had been there a few times before. I made the mistake of trying to correct her. She grew more and more adamant, claiming, "I have never set foot in this place in my life!"

I learned two important lessons that day: Put aside feeling of personal embarrassment, and don't insist upon logic or accuracy.

On one of my visits, she accused me of not writing to her anymore. In my defense, I pointed out a stack of my letters on her dresser. She snapped, "Well, Miss Smarty, if those letters are really from you, why don't you just go ahead and read them to me!" I read one aloud. She listened attentively, laughed now and then, and made fill in comments as though I were someone outside the family requiring further input in order to understand.

Later, a nurse told me, "We read your letters to your Mom again and again. She never gets tired of them, especially the memories." That news inspired me.

When I returned home to Colorado, I began a new batch of letters. Each started, "Dear Mom, Do you remember when ....?" I recalled as many family stories as I could, then plundered our old photo albums for ideas and inspiration, things I hadn't thought about in years. The more I dredged up humorous and memorable events from our mutual pasts, the more enthusiastic I became. In this case, dwelling on the past was serving a worthwhile purpose. It offered an excellent way to tap into the good times, those wonderful times when Mom was creative, loving, and actively involved in our local church and community. Because she was such a persuasive and successful Sunday school teacher, I can still bellow out the lyrics to "Jesus Loves Me," by heart, and believe every word.

Eventually, talking or reading to Mom was like trying to communicate with a ghost. She simply "wasn't there"; nevertheless, I continued reading aloud in her presence, which gave me something to do during long stretches of visiting time.

The letters reminded me that during most of Mom's adult life she made the world a better place. That is how I always will remember her.

DEAR MOM was published originally in GUIDEPOST magazine in May of 2000.

STIERUM*
Shirley Meier

We sit and talk, my mother and I, about the early days on the prairie when she was a little girl. She's now living with us and upon my urging, she tries to remember stories that her ethnic German parents from Russia told as they sat around the pot bellied stove on snowy evenings. She knows they came from the village of Alexanderhilf near Odessa in the Ukraine but she can't recount many specific names or incidents of that world.

"Oh, they talked about swimming in the Dnjester River or the Scharzes Meer (Black Sea)", my mother volunteered. "And Father bragged about their voyage on the ocean. He had been one of the few who didn't suffer sea sickness."

As a child of the North Dakota prairie myself, I could image how big bodies of water must have seemed an incredible mystery to Mother and her siblings, making more of an impression than talks of the Russian steppes. Few of them in their lifetime would see an ocean and the Missouri was the biggest river they knew. They learned to pray for rain water from infancy, but they had little opportunity to learn to swim. My parents even forbade my ever going to our muddy pasture dam because of fear of drowning.

Mother's lapse of memory isn't only due to her advanced age, but as she says, it's the fact that as a youngster she had little interest in unseen faces and places. She'd heard repeated stories of these people who married whom, who didn't marry, who had to marry while her parents sadly remembered bygone friends. They spoke with the affection of things lost forever and also forever embellished, but it was a canvas that my mother couldn't see.

Even the dorf (village), so often recalled, with its neat rows of acacia trees and stucco houses seemed foreign to her. In my mother's world, the New World of the treeless prairie, no neighbor's house could even be seen on the wide horizon. They did have the comfort, however, in knowing that most of their far flung neighbors spoke their language and shared their religious and cultural heritage.

"Did they ever talk about work?" I inquired, knowing that most of them had been small landowners, growing grain in the Black Sea area. Three generations before they had migrated from Germany to Southern Russia, bringing their seeds and knowledge with them. Later, they repeated the same pattern here, taming the Northern Plains and making

24

it the bread basket of America.

"Not much, perhaps because they were young, just newlyweds when they left for America. When our neighbors came to visit Sunday afternoons, they talked a lot about the crops and breaking sod here, getting water to a new pasture, where to get new bulls. That sort of thing. I think those tasks were similar in Russia."

"I remember they were always very subdued when I was a little girl," I said, remembering my many evenings listening to my grandparents' restricted tone.

"But if it was about politics, they got to shouting," Mother laughed.

"Was that about America or Russia? " I asked, knowing Mother's interest in the topic.

"Oh, both, and sometimes about Germany too. The first war was on when I was young and other Americans thought we were real Germans, you know like the Reich Germans. Or some thought of us as Russians, which wasn't as uncomfortable an identity at the time but people feared them too."

I knew that although they had retained much of the German culture and language, in reality they didn't know much about the original Fatherland. I also knew that the generalized stigma against anything German or German-like during the First World War in America had left a definite impression on my mother's generation. Born and educated in the United States, they grew up with different ways and most of them avoided European influences.

Mother sighs now and I can tell she is weary. The rain, such welcome music of the Great Plains, taps on the window. May has been a wet month, bad for her joints but good for the crops. Looking hopefully for the sky to lighten, I long for the sunny air of early June on the prairie. It will come for us, but usually just for a few days before the summer's intense heat hits.

"I wonder how long it's going to rain," I say out loud. It's one side of the eternal prairie chant; the other side is "I wonder how long it's going to snow". Such speculation is natural, especially for those of us who have been married to the soil, dependent on it for a livelihood.

My mother rubs her arms. I reach for a crocheted afghan to cover her because she is old now and frail. Her white hair is curled but thin; her skin, also thin and splotchy, has blue veins raised high on her hands. Eye glasses sit a bit crooked on her nose and her lacy collar gaps open at her throat. The walker with its attached basket, filled with letters, candy and small mail order catalogues, stands waiting in front of her chair.

Our conversation drifts to local gossip, which only marginally amuses her, and she seems too tired for politics today. I need to plan an afternoon activity for her because too much daytime dozing has unbalanced her mental clock, making her restless and rambling at night. She looks at the pictures in the newspaper but loses concentration quickly with reading. We've tried puzzles but she can't do them alone and lately, sewing requires too much effort, mostly from me guiding her.

Over the years she's made countless quilts, the art form of pioneer women, and some of them are on the beds now. Once in a while she'll ask if she made the "trip around the world" one on the wall, my favorite. I tell her that she did and she smiles wistfully. I look at it too, thinking of my family's difficult journeys over the last two hundred years. The comparison of their desire for a better life and my own pleasurable modern travel makes the tiny squares circling the quilt take on added meaning.

I often played the piano for her because she enjoyed it, but I've got too much work to do today. Perhaps listening to a TV talk show or a CD will be entertaining. My collection of "oldies" probably won't work as they are based on jazz or early rock and roll. Better stick with light classical, a favorite of both hers and mine, or some folk music. Easy listening like Lawrence Welk might do.

She breaks the silence. "What are we going to eat tonight? It's a good sign as her appetite is almost non existent. "Make it simple," she says in her plaintive voice. "You don't have to fuss over me."

I sigh in concentration. "Let's fix something old fashioned. You can help me. How about stierum?"

"Yes, if that's what you want. I haven't had it in a long while."

Stierum is a family favorite, our comfort food, but I haven't made it in a long time either. As an egg dough mixture, somewhat a cross between scrambled eggs and pancakes, it comes with numerous names. Many ethnic groups served it as a substitute for potatoes or rice. On hot summer days, I love to sprinkle stierum with bacon bits or pieces of sausage, serve it with fresh milk and creamed lettuce from the garden.

Interesting how recipes survive longer than political oration, fashion or even language and religion. Today few of my cousins have much knowledge of German or history of our ethnic ancestors, but the eating habits are still engrained in us. Assimilation has worked well for us and while I highly value my heritage, I often question the intolerance that isolated language and religion brings to people.

26

"Tell me, again, Mom. How do you make that?" I lie in my question.

"Oh, you know. Eggs, some milk or cream, little flour. You modern girls just don't seem to remember even the easiest recipes."

Smiling, I take the modern girl reference as a compliment, even though I'm retirement age. Getting the bowls out, I start to assemble the ingredients. I ask her to beat four eggs, after I added a dash of salt and a cup of two percent milk. In the old days, before our concern about cholesterol, we never thought twice about using cream, the real reason it truly did taste better in our memories.

"Here, let me finish this," I say a few minutes later, noticing that she has stopped mixing. After staring at me for a long moment, she surrenders the bowl to me. I add flour, unmeasured, from the canister, but enough to make a thick dough. It requires a good twist of the wrist to combine and whip it about. Later, I'll pour the stierum into a hot oiled iron pan, frying the mixture and turning it while also chopping it into big bite sized pieces.

Looking at her hands, I remember with a twinge, those same hands kneading dough, peeling potatoes, making meals, not only for our family, but for a threshing crew of ten or twelve. That was all in a day's work then and now she deserves her rest I feel. However, she isn't enjoying, understanding or accepting her freedom from labor. The conflict between wanting to do things and not being able had become her true crippler.

"I learned about stierum when I was young," she muses.

"So did I," I add but she doesn't hear me. I make a mental note to fix a batch the next time my grown daughters come home to visit.

Mother is nodding off again, perhaps reaching back to her childhood, to her own mother. My grandmother had surely always been old, standing with her knotted hair in front of a wood stove in the detached shed which served as their summer kitchen. She made stierum on hot days too, I'm sure.

Mom's probably now remembering stumbling across the grasslands toward the country school, scrubbing clothes on the washboard, or giggling with girl friends during confirmation class. Pictures of rippling wheat field on windy summer days may fill her mind along with men in patched overalls marching home from the fields, their dry short laughter crackling in the air. Perhaps too that young man's face, my father, as he rode his pinto into their yard, waving his hat, bring gusto and love to her.

Later she stirs and wakens. "It must be time to eat." She sounds stronger and happier. I pour the stierum dough into the iron fry pan. It sizzles. Meanwhile, the rain stops and the sun breaks through the clouds.

STIERUM first appeared in the JOURNAL of the AMERICAN HISTORICAL SOCIETY JOURNAL of Germans from Russia in 2000.

BUT, IS IT ART?

Claire L. Brown

Artists are causing a stir
With abstractions resembling a `whirr.'
      Can viewers be thrilled
      When a canvas is filled
With a splatter, a blotch, and a blur?

      `White on white' can be highly confusing;
      The general public is left bemusing.
            They would try and try
            To understand why
      The artist thought it amusing.

            Viewers began to berate
            A sculpture resembling a crate.
                  "It shows deep conjecture,"
                  Was claimed during a lecture,
            Which fostered a `hot' debate.

            A wild eyed artist named Herman
            Depicted humans as vermin.
                  He raved, "Please repent
                  Before life is spent!"
            He felt he was painting a sermon.

                  An artist called Claude Monet
                  Could paint the essence of day;
                        But I sense paranoia
                        When I gaze at a Goya,
                  So I try Corot or Courbet.

THE BRACELET
Jeanne Freed

My hand reached forward and instantly pulled back stinging with my anguish. I knew I had to do it. But, perhaps it was too soon. I wondered if I'd be thought of as callous or cold hearted. Suddenly I knew that something so much a part of her must be a part of me. Again I reached toward her pale thin wrist. Gently, with trembling fingers I removed the golden circle from her arm. Then I kissed her goodbye for the last time.

My mother wore the gold bangle bracelet for as long as I could remember. It was as much a part of her as her wedding ring or her fragrance of rose water. It never occurred to me to ask why she wore it or where it came from. I only knew I had to do the same.

At first, I was acutely aware of its presence banging it against walls, catching it in my sleeves and hooking it on every drawer pull. Every minute nerve in my arm sensed its movement. Though the bracelet itself was only ounces, it weighed so heavily upon me.

It became omnipresent. Each little jangle pealed like cathedral bells, reminding me constantly of her. Memories flashed off its patina and I often envisioned my mother's luminescent hand and graceful fingers forever etched into the gold

In spite of its awkward perch, it was strangely comforting. Sometimes it captured the warmth of the sun, and a sensation of her tender touch embraced me. The cold of winter would often chill the metal and I'd feel a shiver of loss and grief. The bracelet was both guardian angel and sentinel.

As years passed, the bracelet became part of me. It traveled down the aisle and listened as I repeated my marriage vows. Our bracelet reflected the heat of my body as I labored through the birth of my daughters. Since the day my mother died, our bracelet has heard every word I uttered and been every place I've been. The same felt true for my mother.

Recently, a longtime friend took notice of our bracelet. After explaining I hadn't been without it for a very long time, she was genuinely surprised. It seemed ironic and yet appropriate. A small circlet, unbroken and unending, binds us in a fashion no one else can see. Mom would love that.

IT'S THE LITTLE THINGS...*

Claire L. Brown

I was well into a good book, semi reclined, comfy in slippers, and sipping my first cup of coffee for the day when I was jangled back into reality by a lawn mowing crew next door. Listening to their buzzing and clanking back and forth, I realized that our yard would be next. Then it occurred to me that our garden hoses had been left strung out across the grass, and needed to be moved in order for them to mow. Should I do it? ...or shouldn't I? I would rather remain exactly where I was, and why not? "It's not a big issue. It's a little insignificant thing," I mused, as I slouched farther down in my comforter. "Besides, they get paid for it,"

Then 1 made the dastardly error of putting myself in their place, and facing the fact that a routine job could be made easier and faster if they weren't forced to contend with errant hoses.

I dragged my phlegmatic disheveled early morning self across the lawn, gathered up the pesky snake like creatures, wound them into coils, and dropped them on the patio to sleep in the sun. The entire non dramatic scenario involved about four minutes.

As I returned to my book and coffee, it dawned on me that only yesterday the church service had included something about doing small random acts of kindness. Today was Monday.

Had I forgotten already?

*IT'S THE LITTLE THINGS THAT COUNT was published in GLAD TIDINGS, Greenwood Village, Colorado, May 2004.

HOLIDAY MEMORIES*
Shirley Meier

Clickety clack, clickety clack went the rhythmic, metallic sound of the train's wheels. Jingle jangle was the ringing of the little silver bells on my coat lapel. As I stood and swayed, they were in perfect synchronism: a rolling beat augmenting my own heart's refrain, "going, going, going home for the holidays."

Home for me at Christmas was still North Dakota, even though I was newly married and living near Chicago. It was a long train trip and my husband and I had already been standing a couple of hours, caught in the corridor across from the toilet. It was as far as we got when boarding because the train was overbooked and, even with reservations, the choice was to stand or stay behind.

The farm lands of Illinois, with the corn rows standing straight, disappeared as we came to the Mississippi. From our position we could only peek out diagonally and see the river with the winding train tracks beside it. The quick afternoon sun, sending long shadows from the trees, descended and we continued on with clickety clack, jingle jangle. We were tired, but we smiled a lot for it was an adventure, packed with people on each side of us. Everywhere there were packages, cases, and festive wrappings.

We stood all the way to Minneapolis. However, then the great crunch of people left and we found a seat in the coach, giggling and poking one another to see if we were still alive. My husband stowed our bags and I ran out to the depot for sandwiches. Back in the train, we ate them in one motion and fell into an exhausted sleep. We didn't hear the clickey clack, now a more muffled cadence, as the locomotive swept onward in the dark.

I awoke with a start as the conductor announced Fargo. The coach was dark now and the moonlight showed the flat white landscape of Western Minnesota as it met the Red River country. Almost in Dakotaland! Such a land of space and freedom for those of us who knew it. Glancing outside, I could see the blurry crimson color of the Northern Lights and straining upward, I could see the clear sparkle of stars.

I didn't go back to sleep. I started to name the towns, all familiar stops, miles and miles distant from one another but all bringing us closer to home. Valley City, Jamestown, soon Bismarck. Bismarck was our stop, even though home was still another hour away. But that didn't matter.

Then we were finally there with my father's hearty laugh, Mom's gentle embrace, and my husband's more vibrant conversation. It was now early morning, an awfully cold time. The wind was brisk and our chatter bounced in echo up the frozen street as we hustled to the car. We sat tightly together, engulfed with our coats and luggage, wiggles and squeezes. Driving out of town across the Missouri toward the West River country, we saw the empty pristine prairie was sparkling with new snow as the sun came up.

However, as we neared the ranch with the ones I loved, my world was full and toasty warm.

*HOLIDAY MEMORIES appeared in the N.W. SUBURBAN HERALD (Chicago), 1988.

TRIBUTE TO COAST GUARD'S COWSLIP
(a memorable Coast Guard Cutter)
Claire L. Brown

The Cowslip has been a favorite
Of many a sailor at sea,
For her well earned reputation,
And her comradery.

Whenever called to duty
The Cowslip flew into gear.
Her ever valiant performance
Compels us to be here.

`Semper paratis' has been the guide
For crews ever loyal and brave.
Of these men we are highly proud,
So let the banners wave!

This poem was read by the captain of the Cowslip, Lt.Cmdr. Hal R. Pitts, at her decommissioning ceremony at Tongue Point, Astoria, Oregon. She had served well for an amazing sixty years. The poem also was published in the Littleton Independent newspaper in conjunction with a feature story of the occasion.

The Cowslip was built in Duluth, Minnesota, under the direction of the President of the Marine Iron and Shipbuilding Co., Arnold W. Leraan. His daughter, Claire Leraan Brown, coincidently was present at both the initial launching in April, 1942, and at the decommissioning in December, 2002. She found the most recent occasion refreshingly patriotic.

HEE HAW

CLOVERLESS

An earthy young woman from Dover
In summer wore only clover.
Then when came fall
She wore nothing at all
For the clover season was over.

Claire L. Brown

(IT'S A KICK) LIMERICKS

Claire L. Brown

CELL PHONES

There once was a phone called a `cell,'
Whose ring was a signal from hell.
    I may seem a prude,
    But in restaurants they're rude.
How can the user not tell?

        Put down your cell phone and drive.
           We want to remain alive.
           Your vehicles' veering
        From lack of good steering;
        While the rest of us try to survive.

OLD FLAME

        I remember my dear old flame,
        But I hardly recall his name.
           Whether dull or wise
           A glowing spark dies.
        Only cold ashes remain.

ON VACATION

        Geese doing their honking oration
        Flew in triangular formation.
           The ones in back
           Were slower and slack.
        I notice these things on vacation.

MY UFO*
Jeanne Freed

I always wanted to see a UFO. Nothing up close and personal. . .no abductions or little gray men, just a simple unidentified flying object.

Over the span of numerous camping trips, sitting around the old campfire and staring up at the spectacular Milky Way, I couldn't help but wonder why I never saw anything I couldn't rationalize. Some specks of light were radiant red or pale pinks, while others blinked yellow and blue. Fast moving dots of light were almost certainly satellites or high flying jets. The smaller bouncing lights were easily identified in the catch all category of atmospheric conditions and light refraction. To my way of thinking, a true unknown object would have to either have distinctive shape or behave erratically.

Staring at the night sky did have its advantages though, because in New Mexico, I am sure I got a good look at the Space Shuttle in orbit. In Wyoming, as dusk settled in near a reservoir, I watched a jet refueling from a huge tanker. I never would have seen them if I hadn't been paying attention.

I finally saw a UFO. But, not in the wilderness, and not because I was actively looking. No, my UFO was viewed in the suburbs, out my back door at 6: 10 am in the middle of December.

I'd been downstairs long enough to get a cup of coffee, let our dogs out, and turn on the morning news show. My body clock requires a little snatch of wake up time before the furious flurry of getting my daughters off to school, and this was my routine, done hundreds of times before.

It was still very dark out, and as usual I glanced toward the door to see if my wimpy dogs were standing there pleading to come back in. But my attention was drawn to a bright, soupy green light moving quickly across the sky to the north. The shape was elliptical with bright filmy tendrils staggered about the perimeter. My first thought was a search beacon or headlight reflecting off the houses. But before I could form a whole thought, the light stopped moving and seemed to dissolve into itself.

The duration of my sighting was probably under ten seconds. My lips barely had the time to mouth the words, "What the heck was that?"

Excited, I was anxious to share my experience with the first available human. In my case it was my teenage daughter.

"Guess what?" I said to her as she stomped down the stairs in her usual hostile early morning temperament.

"What?" she replied snappishly.

"I just saw a UFO."

"Oh yeah."

"Yeah, it was this weird green light and then it just disappeared."

"What was it?"

"If I knew that, then I wouldn't have called it a UFO."

She was definitely not as impressed as I would have liked, and the conversation dwindled after that. I was quickly learning that my experience would not be as satisfying as originally thought. The problem inherent to a sighting, is there was not an answer to the "what the heck was that?"question. Wishing to see a UFO and actually seeing one turns out to be a hollow victory.

Still, I hoped the news team on television would suddenly look alert and say, "This just in, a breaking new story!" But of course they didn't.

Next, I told my husband. His first response was the perfunctory, "Oh yeah?" Then he looked very serious and said something about swamp gas trapped in a weather balloon reflecting light off of Jupiter.

"What are you talking about?" I asked, thoroughly dumfounded.

Smiling, he said, "Don't you remember, that was a line from MEN IN BLACK."

I was a little miffed until I realized how typical it was for him to use a line from a movie. His head was filled with memorable quotes waiting to be used. But, once he got that out of his system, I think he truly believed me, but didn't think my encounter was any big deal. After all, I was still there, and I hadn't grown an extra head or added a third eye to the back of my neck.

Since the morning news let me down, I decided to keep my eyes and ears open for the next couple of days. I scoured the daily newspaper and stayed up later than usual, checking for news on all the local stations. Either nobody else saw it, or they were also keeping a low profile.

After giving myself a thorough mental check up, I declared myself competent and hallucination free. But I had to accept the fact that I was now "one of them", that strange little group of presumed whackos who saw "something".

I decided I had to tell my best friend. After she got the "Oh yeah?" out of her system, she was quite open minded. Naturally, we managed to turn a few seconds of light in the sky into a nearly two hour conversation, that ended with my sincerest wishes that she would see something strange too.

Next I told my brother. "Oh yeah?" he said. Always the family skeptic, he asked me numerous questions. I wanted badly to elaborate and make my little sighting into something of major importance, but I knew there wasn't much I could add without lying. My brother accepted my information, and with very few negative comments. However, for the next several days, he delighted in leaving messages from "aliens" on my answering machine.

The only good part of this experience, is that now whenever there is a show about sightings, I get to mutter things like, "mine didn't look like that," or " that's the right color, but the shape is wrong,"

I've pretty much resigned myself to never knowing what it was. Maybe it will happen again, or maybe it won't. I only know, that I don't know "what the heck it was".

*MY UFO first appeared in THE DENVER POST 2000

Claire L. Brown

AN HERBAL GERBIL

My pet vegetarian gerbil
Was neither wise nor verbal.
    He moved with stealth,
    Was obsessed with health,
Preferring foods green and herbal.

A LEVEL WORLD

My neighbor, the strange Mr. Revill
Carried a slide rule and bevel
    He measured and puttered,
    And constantly muttered.
He wanted his world to be level.

FACE LIFT

She had a face lift while off on a spree
Her new appearance filled her with glee.
    I won't make her mad,
    Though it seems rather sad;
She looks much the same to me.

MY UNCLE INGVALD

Claire L. Brown

Even when alone my Uncle Ingvald does nothing quietly. He blows his nose, sniffing in between honks, coughs a few times, clears his throat as if preparing for a speech, and offers up an occasional `hum' or `hmm.' As a high school student I nicknamed him, "S.O.S.," standing for "Series Of Sounds." I meant no harm by it, keeping the nickname to myself.

At the breakfast table Ingvald is at his resonant best with eating noises echoing in a culinary chorus, still, of course, by himself. He has a way of turning everyday toast consumption into a surprisingly colorful enterprise. After the toaster lever is pressed down with a snap, the toast soon pops up and up, landing on the table top in front of him. Rather than repair it, he finds it amusing. His repetitious crunching is loud enough to discourage any lurking burglar.. Naturally, he prefers foods which generate sound more easily, such as dry cereal or well done English muffins. Cereals that snap, crackle or pop are special, but are eaten quickly before being softened by added milk.

Eating soup merits audible slurps with each spoonful, followed by `mmm' when it's to his liking. If by chance it isn't to his liking, one still hears the slurps, but the `mmms' are noticeably absent.

Whenever bacon is included in Ingvald's menu, he prefers it well done and crisp. He cuts it politely with his knife and fork, producing a slight grating sound, which precedes the clink of his silverware onto the plate. Before finishing a meal, one or other of the utensils usually plinks on the floor. His chair scrapes in sliding back from the table to retrieve it, and then again in return.

As Ingvald carries his cup of coffee over to the couch, there is soon to be heard a cadence of slurp clink slurp clink, followed eventually by a low subtle belch. He reads the morning newspaper as if a breeze were blowing in from his screen door causing rustling and rattling. Finally, he folds the paper, slaps it against the side of his leg (an innocent enough habit), then drops it into the wastebasket with a thud of finality.

The clanking of dishes as he carries them to the sink rivals that of any busy restaurant. It could be that Ingvald regards any activity which is inaudible as less worthwhile to perform. I don't know, and wouldn't dream of asking. As he leaves the room to get dressed for the day, two or three sneezes can be heard, not to mention muffled motor boat like unidentifiable rumbles.

Ingvald defnitely enjoys the sounds of his own presence. He feels accompanied, on good terms with the world, and at odds with nothing or no one. He never has to ask the popular generic question, "Who am I?" Obviously, he is a living, breathing, analytical sound machine set in slow motion. In his present senior life style everything blends in harmonious cacophony, as of course, it should. Why Not?

Being popular, Ingvald often meets friends for lunch, or is invited out for dinner. He is a clever conversationalist, smart dresser, intelligent (if not quite handsome) in appearance, and has impeccable table manners. Fortunately, he makes fewer personal noises when in society than when alone. At least, no one ever has commented on the matter to my knowledge.

Never have I heard any hostess say, "I left croutons off the dinner salad in order not to listen to Ingvald masticate," or, "I'm serving a perfectly noiseless dessert since Ingvald will be joining us." However, if wine is offered with dinner, Uncle Ingvald eventually can be counted upon to hiccup, not just once, and not overly loud, but certainly hearable from a distance of four or five feet. I'm the only one who smiles when he hics`. Others politely pretend not to notice. Come to think of it, maybe they really don't.

Rest assured, Ingvald will never overstay his welcome. He hears the mystical, but insistent call of his pajamas around 9:00 p.m. They expect him home and tucked in by 9:30 p.m., and he never fails them.

Frankly, after all is said and done, I enjoy visiting Uncle Ingvald since he retired. He is well read, inspiring to talk with, and I can always tell whether or not he is at home without having to ring the bell. I simply listen for familiar sounds through the open screen door.

yet more LIMERICKS...

Claire L. Brown

LEARN THE LANGUAGE

A warrior in Santa Domingo,
A truly high spirited Gringo,
    Meant to vanquish the land
    In a manner quite grand,
But he never could conquer the lingo.

NO CLONING TODAY

Advances in animal cloning
Breeders are lately postponing,
    Having produced a poor copy
    Looking sickly and sloppy,
For which they are now bemoaning.

OVERDOING IT

I knew a "veggie" nut named Barrett,
    Whose favorite food was a carrot.
    His verve did fail
    As he became frail.
He died sharing food with his parrot.

GROW UP*
Jeanne Freed

My daughter has asked for her first bra. I should have been prepared. Mothers are supposed to tune in to their daughters' maturing needs. Maybe I would have if the aforementioned child hadn't just recently started to wiggle her first loose baby tooth, and is only six years old. However, she's absolutely convinced her breasts are budding, often posing and running her little hand down the length of her imagined hourglass figure. I have the urge to procrastinate, as I see her shape a little differently.

"Absolutely not," advised my much younger and more progressive sister in law. "You must respond to her womanly demands or you will forever repress her sexuality."

I fail to see the awakening sexuality of my little progeny. She prefers panties decorated with Disney characters, and just last week was perfectly happy to wear pink cotton undershirts. But hey, she'd just started kindergarten.

"Get her a sports bra,"advised by sister in law. "It will help her self esteem."

So I purchased a tiny sports bra, the equivalent of half an undershirt at twice the price. But my daughter loves the bra; and has a happy, contented appreciation of her figure. However, like a Victoria's Secret model, she prefers wearing it sans shirt, with a ruffled skirt, dress shoes, and a feather boa.

Is this a portent of the future? Will she soon want to shave the pale, downy fuzz on her spindly little legs, begging for a bikini wax on her seventh birthday and bodice ripping fiction for bedtime reading?

Of course this progression is being closely watched by my older daughter, "The Prude". She is nearly ten and much closer to the bloom of womanhood, but she's the kind of girl who will not consider wearing a two piece bathing suit and shudders at the thought of a sleeveless blouse. She started using safety pins to secure her Peter Pan collars when she was only three. Nobody was ever going to sneak a glance down her blouse.

"I can't believe you bought her a bra, Mother," she stated with a tone of vast superiority.

"But her budding womanhood must be reinforced," I countered. "Maybe you should have a bra, too." I figured I'd better not repress this daughter either, or the blame would be boundless.

"Get real, Mother. Like I have anything. . . how embarrassing" At

45

this point, she stomped away, glaring at me over her shoulder.

My oldest ... so logical... so mature. I better watch her closely.

Will I continue to quell one daughter's sexuality while I turn the other into a puritanical turtleneck wearer? Does all this mean I am doomed to raise one teenage daughter's illegitimate children while the other daughter goes on to spinsterhood, highlighted by a career in the Department of Motor Vehicles?

While I ponder our future, the little bra wearer shows up. "Mom, we need to talk in private."

Oh no! It's time for the big sex talk, and I'm not prepared!

She holds out her hand showing a miniscule baby tooth. "How exactly, is the Tooth Fairy going to get in the house since it's locked up for winter?" This question I can handle.

GROWUP first appeared in HARPOON 1995

LIMERICKS ad infinitum...

Claire L. Brown

FOUR WHEEL PERSONALITY

Toward his sports car I show no disdain.
His emotional attachment is plain.
    Since there's not room for much,
    Like golf clubs and such,
I'd sooner ride in a train.

WHAT WAS IT?

A tiny plant was determined to grow
Up through melting spring snow.
        Was it a lily?
        Don't be silly.
T'was the maianthemem canadenso.

WE LEFT

Invariably my friend showed up late
For appointments or any type date.
        Never taking the blame,
        Her excuses were lame
'Til she learned we would no longer wait.

IT'S GONE

I discovered a trail with a twist
My skis simply couldn't resist;
        But the wind caused a stir.
        The scene was a blur,
And the rest of the trail I missed.

TOO CLOSE FOR COMFORT*
Claire L. Brown

I was headed out of town in a hurry, being late for an important appointment. Well, actually, I was on my way to meet a couple of old high school friends for lunch, an exciting prospect since we hadn't seen each other in close to three years.

My mind was happily occupied with all the silly antics we pulled, which we thought at the time were so clever.

It suddenly dawned on me that I was passing a police car. Since it was traveling the speed limit, obviously, I wasn't, not by a long shot. What an unexpected jolt! I moaned to myself, realizing that a speeding ticket was the last thing I needed, my last one having been only a month earlier. What could I say or do? "Ohh no, I'm done for," I decided .....unless...think... , think.

Glaring strobing lights guided me over to the side of the road while passers by craned their necks to see what was happening. I took a deep breath as I watched the officer step out of his car, and walk briskly up to mine. He appeared at least eight feet tall with piercing eyes like a charging bull about to do battle.

I lowered my window with a hint of a forced smile, and said, "I'll bet I know why you pulled me over. You want to sell me tickets to the Policemen's Ball. Right?"

Straight faced, he retorted quickly and officially, "Policemen don't have balls!"

I tittered, placing my hand over my mouth in lady like surprise. "Oh?" was all I could utter.

The policeman's face broke into an embarrassed grin. He shook his head. After giving me a short admonition on my excessive speed, and driving skills in general, he stepped back for me to leave, un-ticketed, but humbly repentant.

*TOO CLOSE FOR COMFORT was published in the SUMMIT COUNTY (CO.) INDEPENDENT, 8/03.

WHAT KIND OF SQUIRREL AM I?

Jeanne Freed

Finally I'm ready. First paragraph, first sentence. How hard can it be to write a novel?

Yolanda walks slowly through the woods, her mind searching for hidden meaning in the words of her argument with Alessandro.

Good prose needs visual flavor I remind myself.

She pauses to watch a squirrel run up a tree.

Since my reader must envision through my words, I decide to elaborate on the little critter. What are those dark colored squirrels with the tufty ears called? Hmm . . . Maybe there's something in the old encyclopedia. No, not the forest friend I'm picturing. "Wildlife of North America"? Not there either. Obviously my home library is lacking. Seeing no alternative, I save my two sentences to disk and go online.

I have new mail and a good offer on panties from Victoria's Secret. Thirty minutes later, I key in a search for squirrels. National Geographic has an interesting article on Peruvian mummies and a taste bud experiment, so I make it to the mammal page forty two minutes later and locate "Family Sciuridae".

I didn't know ground squirrels looked so much like chipmunks. But where is my fuzzy tuft eared friend? Not a Douglas, Gray, Red, Niger (very cute), Abert's, but finally a Kaibab. I was hoping for a more familial name like Candy Tuft, or Feather Ears. Maybe a different squirrel would be better. I really like the Niger. Says it is indigenous to Texas though, my character lives in Wisconsin. Maybe nobody will notice.

She smiles as the acrobatic black Niger squirrel scampers up the large tree.

Hmm... better expound on the tree. A majestic oak? A sturdy maple? A quaking aspen?

What do they have in Wisconsin? Hmmm...

Seeing no other choice, I save my three sentences to a disk and go back online.

WITHOUT A HITCH

BOLDNESS BACKFIRES

There once was a mean mule from Dover
Whose herder was bold as a rover.
One day for a joke
He yanked on the rope.
Now he lies deep beneath clover.

Claire L. Brown

IMPATIENT GARDENER*

Claire L. Brown

In the throes of winter I find myself
Gazing wistfully across my lawn.
The urge to dig and plant
Postponed 'til snow is gone.

Flowerbeds overgrown with weeds,
And soil determinedly hard,
Still beckon me as temperatures rise
For a stroll around the yard.

Bugs and insects have burrowed in
Waiting out hard frost and cold.
Are they dreaming dreams beneath the soil?
Come spring they'll be more bold.

I'm having endless visions
Of flowers glorious and profuse;
Yet glancing at brownish grass and leaves,
I know it's of no use.

Thumbing through seed catalogs
Is an annual rite I can't forego.
My husband quips, "Relax, my dear.
The forecast portends more snow."

*IMPATIENT GARDENER won acceptance in the INTERNATIONAL LIBRARY
OF POETRY in November of 2000, and can be located on the Internet under
claireleraanbrown@www.poetry.com.

MOOD OF A MEXICAN TOWN*
Shirley Meier

I first felt the Mexican spirit in Guaymas
Where California Bay sweeps its sultry breezes
Almost undefined across the expectant harbor
To modern buildings rising from fishing rubble.

From a day of desert and arid apprehensiveness
I came to salt water with boats rocking quietly.
Far out in the west, a bolt of white lightning
Pointed with thin fingers to the morrow's catch.

Sitting on the balcony, watching the crowd below
I saw men in worn sandals and stained shirts
Quietly strolling past with hunched old women
Covered with black mantillas and faithfulness.

At the street's end, sat strong swarthy men
Weary after a day of fishing with the gringo
Lazily joking and drinking cold Corona beer
Ever watching for signs of swishing skirts.

I heard a vender's monotonous high voice
The creaking of his cart and small tinkling bell
The clip clopping of the laden burro's hooves
Echoing up stone streets and walled gardens.

Through a patio, fringed with lacy bougainvillea
Came a boy in tattered pants selling chiclets
His bare feet sliding along smooth glazed tile
A shy smile escaping while taking our centavos.

A bronzed Indian woman was cooking corn and beans
And the smoke from her wood curled and drifted
Past me and the balcony, swirling upward, around,
Brushing, caressing the stoic cathedral's face.

And suddenly from a nearby unseen restaurant
In a mariachi song of exclamation and revolution
Came the sound of a skilled, clear, quick trumpet
Sending its vibrant soul far out into the night.

*MOOD of a MEXICAN TOWN, a 1990 winning entry in SALUTE to the ARTS at Triton (IL) College, also appeared in the NAT. POETRY ANTHOLOGY in 1983.

CROSS COUNTRY SKIING
Claire L. Brown

White cloaked vistas
Obliterating summer's green
See tiny pussy willow buds
Peeking out upon the scene.

Exhilarated to the maximum,
I'm attuned to nature's way.
Skis push powdery snow aside
On a cool crisp sunny day.

As the winding trail slants upward
I lean forward into the hill
With skis fanned out in herringbone,
Edges crunch against their will.

Tired and gasping at the summit,
I gaze my time away
At panoramas stretching forth
In glistening white array.

A mystical journey back home
Through wedding cake terrain.
Winter's end approaches soon,
And I'll return again.

WINDOWS
Jeanne Freed

The view from my little girl bedroom was the south wall of the house next door. But that house belonged to my grandparents, so the sight of the gray clapboard exterior was always comforting. A circular window stared back at me like a giant's eye from their dormer bedroom. It was the kind of window from which one almost expected to see Rapunzel's hair unfurl while the handsome prince waited below.

When I was in my grandparent's house, despite warnings to be cautious, it felt daring and defiant to poke my head through the open hole, knowing if I leaned too far I could easily tumble to the ground.But I loved to fling open the window and stare down at the driveway below. Swung wide with no screen or barrier to the outside, I could lean out and look down upon the roof of my father's prized 1952 Plymouth, and watch bees frenetically buzz the hollyhocks in my mother's garden. Perched in the window, I was a princess in the tower, awaiting rescue by a knight in shining armor.

When I was about six, my grandparents moved into town to be closer to their business and the house was rented. I was crushed by the loss of their presence and secretly saddened by losing access to my magical window. But my grandparents were both wise and thoughtful, choosing new tenants with a daughter my age.

Though we became fast friends, envy brewed in my heart when Debby moved into the dormer bedroom. I wanted to find faults in my new friend, but Debby was adventurous, funny, didn't mind my interest in the window and readily accepted my explanation. Together we embellished on fairy tales and took turns being Rapunzel, while the other pretended to be the prince calling from below. We fought wizards and dragons, and protected the princess from imagined evils breeching our castle walls.

Often, after we were sent to bed for the night, Debby and I would open our windows and whisper secretly across the span between the houses. Better still, when I was confined to my room for disciplinary purposes, I had an immediate line of outside communication. Though I'm sure it couldn't have been constant, I clearly remember bouts with the croup and being confined in my room with a vaporizer. Usually a pebble would bounce off the windowpane, and there was Debby making silly faces, and wild pantomimes to ease my boredom.

Time passed, Debby moved and we also moved into town., My

grandparents kept the house and in between tenants I was able to visit, always heading right for the bedroom to stick my head out. Though my enchanted window grew smaller as I grew older, it always reminded me of a time of imagination, when little a girl dreamed of princes and dragons, princesses and fairy tales. The magic of those halcyon days will never cease, because I won't forget the little dormer window in my beloved grandparents home.

IT MUST BE SPRING

Claire L. Brown

A grey blanket of fog, residue from early morning rain,
Gives new life to sprigs sprouting on gnarled trees.
As fog lifts slowly, moisture remains
Glistening from pools in water soaked fields.

Soft rain drops smugly floating down in mirth
Spread ripples through puddles once serene.
Winds coax scents from sodden earth
To permeate the freshened scene.

Parading clouds break ranks, allowing sunbeams through
To dry the dewy dampened morn.
Buds cast off confining masks,
Displaying beauty in unfolding bloom.

A beckoning call to each living thing,
Awake! Awake! It must be spring.

BRAYING
(Haiku)
Shirley Meier

RAINBOW
Sky arched with color
Brief beauty, vibrant symbol–
Nature's own Haiku.

FLOWERS
Glorious blossoms
Proud, rotund, praising faces–
Heavy in the dirt.

STREAMS
They gurgle and gush
Flow hard to refresh the land–
Litter floats gratis.

SNOW
Serene, elegant
Yet heavy, blinding, frosty–
A grand dame's mantle.

AVALANCHE
Pike's Peak, Hood, Rainier,
Alluring, bigger than life–
Hikers, please take note.

STORM
Whispering, whistling
Wind howling into a gale–
Like gossip rips hearts.

RAINBOWS OVER LAKE DILLON*
Claire L. Brown

Driving along the Dillon dam road on the way to our mountain cabin, I happened to glance over the long stretch of water, unconsciously scanning for sailboats. To my surprise and delight, vague colors in an arch-like shape gradually formed a brilliant rainbow. As I smiled at nature's elegant display, another band of colors began to form yet another rainbow, slightly above the first.

"Fantastic," I thought. "Maybe this is my reward for driving the speed limit."

Deciding to watch the heavenly phenomena for a moment or two, I pulled off the road near the water's edge. While lowering my window to see more clearly, a third smaller rainbow appeared, barely hovering above the still water. I stared in amazement, hypnotized by the strange and glorious sight. Stepping out of the car in a slight drizzle, I shut the door as quietly as possible, as though I were fearful the noise might frighten the scene away.

Other cars began pulling over. One tall smiling fellow in a western hat marveled at the dramatic show of color, then could be heard mumbling to his passenger that neither one of them had a camera or binoculars! We all gathered at the best vantage spot, pointing in awe, and speaking in hushed voices; why, I couldn't say for certain, but the rarified atmosphere seemed to call for quieter tones.

A damp looking be-spectacled kid, stopping on his mountain bike, was full of `ooos' and `ahhhs.' He asked those of us within earshot if we realized that all rainbows have the same identical colors, and are always in the same order. Before anyone could answer, he exclaimed, "See? Red, orange, yellow, green, blue, and violet. It's all caused by the bending refraction and reflection of rays of light from drops of rain in the part of the sky opposite to the sun."

Duly impressed by this spontaneous outdoor classroom enlightenment, I asked, "Have you been studying these things in science class?"

"Yeah," he quipped, "but Mrs. Bogarth will never believe me when I tell her about this once in a lifetime awesome sight. She thinks my imagination works overtime as it is!"

Just as he was giving a resigned sigh, a bright red jeep drove up, spewing dirt and dust as it jerked to a halt. A heavily made up face yelled out her window like a screech owl, "What's everybody `gawkin' at? Did a boat flip over or "somethin'? Huh?"

The quiz kid on the bike chuckled, and said, "No, nothing like that. We...."

The screech owl promptly slammed her car door, and flew off down the road.

He gasped in disbelief. "I don't think she even saw the rainbows!" He walked his bike along the shore, still shaking his head as he waved good bye.

I remained there gazing in fascination until the last wispy remnants of color dissipated slowly into the enveloping mist. During the remainder of my drive to the cabin I had to wonder how many times I may have missed experiencing something inspiring and stupendous, simply because I was in too great a hurry.

*RAINBOWS OVER LAKE DILLON was published in the SUMMIT COUNTY (COLORADO) INDEPENDENT, 12103

BURDENED BURROS

BREEZE

Unseen but moving,
Blowing leaves along path ways
–So travels our fate.

Shirley Meier

SOME EIGHTY YEARS
Shirley Meier

She was born, some eighty years ago,
And now I'm far away.
Yes, I could call, or mail a gift.
But then what would that say?
That I remembered or I didn't forget
The celebration of her day?

I could send a bright potted plant
Or perhaps a cheery bouquet.
But I might wonder, even doubt it,
If that would be the way
To really honor or praise her
On this very important day.

She's old and really needs so little
Friends would often say,
Of course, I'll send a card, but...
But why do I delay?
Is it that I want to show my love
In a more heartfelt way?

Then the phone rings, loud and long.
Again I tend to waylay
Because I suddenly fear and feel
What the caller might relay,
"Yes, she's very ill, close to dying.
Do come right away."

Now, no need for bows and presents
All so colorful, so gay.
What else can my tribute truly be
But to hurry and pray?
For soon she'll receive a better gift
On that, her eternal birth day.

LAYER CAKE

Jeanne Freed

She knew what everybody said about her. She heard them tittering in the restroom and gabbing in the hallways. "Obsessive," some said. "An embarrassment," said one Miss Snotty Pants.

Maybe it was true, but she didn't see her practicality as a fault. Food should never go to waste. Never. People were starving out there.

She was Althea Cruckmyer, and her parents raised her right. "Food is a gift from God, praise his bounty." Her father said those words at the supper table each and every night. His ritual prayer took place, just seconds before she and her nine siblings scrambled for the nearest plate of food.

"Quickly, my babies," said her Mother, "He who hesitates, is lost." What Mother meant was . . . if you didn't grab for food immediately, there wouldn't be a morsel or crumb to fill your belly.

Food was an important part of life on the farm, and good crops meant life or death in a small rural community. If a season failed, money was scarce and the livestock was seen to first. Some winters, they ate watered down soup from the same stock knucklebone for a week. Other winters they ate like a king in his castle, all plump and proud. Food was everything. It should not be wasted.

Now, she lived in the big city and taught pampered children at a fine Middle School. It nearly drove her crazy. No, it wasn't the teaching; she loved to teach. It was the blatant lack of regard for God's bounty, by staff and student alike.

Althea tried, at first, to salvage the crumpled lunch sacks from the cafeteria barrels. But, there were just too many. She ached over the food the bags still contained. She couldn't even bear to watch the kids and teachers dump the remains of "hot lunch" into the trash bins. It amazed her how they could all be so careful about separating the recyclables, while remaining indifferent to the fruits and breads of the earth.

Of course, staff meetings were different, and she was prepared. Left over doughnuts, cookies, and birthday cakes all found their way into her own personal "leftover bag". She'd made it herself from sturdy tent canvas lined with tear proof vinyl. The bag was large enough to hold two grocery bags worth of food. She kept an assortment of plastic sacks and sandwich bags in a small side pocket, ready to wrap up leftovers. There was always plenty of excess everywhere.

Of course Althea couldn't eat everything herself, but she managed to finish off most of it. In fact, she gained close to seventy pounds in the past two years. She meant to give some to a shelter or someplace, but she was afraid to. Strangers might not have the proper respect for God's bounty. No, it was best to bring it home and store it in her freezer or pantry. She would never waste it. It was a comfort, knowing she'd stockpiled enough food, to avoid a starving winter.

"C'mon Althea, take a chance, it's only a buck." Evelyn Webber waved the little yellow ticket, under Althea's nose trying to tempt her. "The Grand Prize is a Cruise."

Evelyn was the closest Althea came to having a friend. "I don't know, I don't like gambling."

"It's not gambling, it's a fundraiser. Who knows, you might win. You never go anywhere for vacation, what've you got to lose?"

"Oh, Okay. But, I never win anything. I never even won a goldfish at the carnival when I was a kid. My brothers and sisters surely won fifty of them."

"It'only a dollar, you won't even miss it."

Althea had to smile. Evelyn was right. Every now and then, a person had to take a chance. A dollar was a small splurge, but it was a big step for her. She was raised to be practical, but she gave Evelyn a dollar and forgot about it.

Part of a teacher's job was to take turns attending teaching seminars and union meetings. Althea was scheduled to attend the next association seminar at a glitzy downtown hotel. She put on her best dress, curled her dull brown hair and added a slash of pink lipstick to her naturally thin lips. Though honored to represent her school, she'd never been to an event of this magnitude, and didn't have an inkling what to expect.

After checking in, and receiving her nametag, Althea was directed toward the Grand Ballroom. The room was built like a giant atrium of sparkling glass and gleaming metal braces. The floor was a mosaic of the Constellations and Planets swirling about a giant universe.

Buffet tables outlined the room, laden with more food than she'd ever seen. An ice sculpture of intricately carved apples glistened beneath a fountain of fruited punch. Chefs, dressed in starched white uniforms with towering pleated hats, stood attentively, holding well honed carving knives. It was all so elegant, so classy.

She wanted to be classy too, but the food captured her attention. Mountains of mashed potatoes and simmering vegetables crowded an entire table. Prime Rib roasts dripped pink juices from rotisseries. Desserts that she couldn't even begin to name were artfully stacked on twinkling silver trays. She was mesmerized.

After three trips through the buffet line, she'd eaten her fill. She barely heard the honored speakers. Her mind was on the remains of the meals consumed.

Piles and piles of rolls sat in baskets, their crusts hardening under heat lamps. Sorbets and pastries melting under the lights. It was offensive. Such an impractical waste.

Althea couldn't help herself. Her hands automatically opened her "leftover bag". She scurried from buffet table to buffet table scooping everything in sight into her bag. She paid no attention to the server's quizzical looks. She heard none of the tittering from her colleagues. She only knew this food would be thrown away, and she couldn't allow that to happen. Not when people were starving. Not if it could keep her from starving. It wasn't practical.

The jokes died down after a couple of weeks. Some of the kids and teachers still made a great show of moving their lunch away from her when she walked by. Althea was hurt, but she knew in her heart, they simply didn't understand.

While deeply into a discussion on Sacajawea and the Native Americans role in exploration, she didn't hear the voice on the loudspeaker at first. "Miss Crukmyer! Please report to the office immediately!" The voice was obviously Evelyn's and she sounded rather excited.

"Okay children, read chapter twelve in your textbook. I trust you'll be on your best behavior. I'll return shortly." Althea knew her students would chat, but she was fairly certain they'd keep it down so she hurried down the hall to the attendance office.

Evelyn met her at the doorway, with a silly secretive grin. "You're not going to believe it! Get in here and sit down."

Althea shook her head questioningly. She followed Evelyn and sat in a chair by the desk.
"Well, my friend, congratulations. You won. I can't believe it, you won!" Evelyn's voice burst with excited giggles.

"Won what?"

"The raffle. The cruise. You won!"

Althea was speechless. She just stared at Evelyn, her mouth agape.

"It's a seven day cruise to Mexico! All the ports. It'll be fantastic. You've got six months to take it. I suggest Spring Break. Listen hon, you've got to lose some weight. There are tons of eligible men on these things. I knew one woman that hooked up with the Commodore of the ship. She had a blast! Althea, are you listening?"

Althea just stared at her. She heard everything Evelyn said, she just couldn't respond. One sentence did make an impression though. Lose weight. The words sent a shiver down her spine.

"You've got six months to get ready. I'll help you, you can be my gym buddy and we'll do it together. What do you say?"

"Yes," Althea said weakly. Then a surprising prick of determination came over her.

"Super. Might as well start today. First we need to change your habits. I'll come over after school, and we'll work out a plan."

It nearly broke her heart, but she allowed Evelyn to mercilessly purge her freezer and pantry, packing up nearly everything she'd saved. "Are you sure the people at the shelter will eat it?"

"Of course, those people are always starving."

Starving. Mustn't worry then.

For the next six months, Althea followed a strict regimen, overseen by Evelyn. She exercised constantly and joined Jazzercise. She put her "Leftover Bag" in the back of the closet. She signed up with Weight Watchers and took herbal appetite suppressants. The weight poured off. She was down to a respectable size twelve.

The day of departure, she was incredibly excited. The ship was one of the Goddess Line, sleek and modern. Her heart fairly leapt in her chest as she climbed the boarding ramp. She felt great. She even thought she looked great.

Her cabin was small, but very compact and functional. She'd heard that nobody ever spent time in his or her room anyway.

It was time for dinner. Dressing with great care, she donned a new black cocktail dress, high black pumps and small pearl earrings. She was a little afraid of meeting strangers, but determined to have the time of her life.

Her assignment was the second seating in the main dining room at the stem of the ship. The huge crowd of people, already sipping wine and cocktails, astounded her. Trying to appear inconspicuous, she weaved her way toward her assigned table. But something caught her attention. She stopped and stared. Mountains of food. Much, much more than at the hotel. Her chest constricted. Her clothes felt tight and confining.

She hadn't given it any thought. She'd been so disciplined. How stupid. How impractical. Now there was no avoiding it. Excess everywhere.

Fifteen other people were seated at her table. Some young, some old, nice friendly people. Their names didn't register, she just smiled and nodded. She ordered Cornish hen and wild rice. She was trying very hard.

Her glance kept creeping toward everyone else's plate. She had to ask. A waiter was at her elbow. "Excuse me, what happens to all the food left over?"

The others at her table listened for the response, interested. She listened with tightening anticipation.

His English wasn't very good. "De fishes. De fishes gets de food." He shrugged, at a loss for the words for garbage.

Her heart sank. They threw it away. The idea was horrifying.

Dinner finally ended and diners were leaving for the lounge or floorshow. Althea's armpits felt damp and sweaty. She lingered at the table. One hand clenched her napkin, the other reached for some rolls and pats of butter. Her evening bag was small, but she managed.

The stockpile grew in every nook and cranny. Already, she couldn't zip up her cocktail dress. It didn't matter; she'd found a colorful Mu Mu at the gift shop. It was wonderful, so comfortable and roomy.

She was doing what she could, but there was so much more. There had to be a way to get to the real food bounty. The scraps and bits she pilfered, were nothing. Somewhere in the bowels of this ship, was the real excess. It was so impractical, somewhere, people were starving.

She examined a map of the ship. The layout was confusing, but Althea was certain she found the location she wanted. "DISPOSAL FACILITY".

She heard voices echoing from the rear of the room. They sounded youthful and foreign. She slipped in and found temporary concealment behind some barrels. The room was utilitarian, unlike the plush cabins on the floors above.

Althea peered between two barrels, her eyes sweeping the rooms contents. It was all here. Tiered carts held the excess, Pastries and breads, hams and vegetables piled high . . . useless. There was so much, she didn't know where to begin.

Then she saw it. A beautiful German Chocolate layer cake topped with sprinkles and dark chocolate curls. Only two slices missing. NO! Her mind screamed. It was only a day old! The inner slices are still moist! She had to have it.

One of the workers moved the pastry cart toward a cavernous opening. She could hear the roar of the engines and the turmoil of the ships wake. Seagulls hovered beyond the opening swooping and squawking.

The worker began to place the pastries on a narrow conveyor belt. One by one cream puffs, eclairs and dainty petit fours disappeared.

She couldn't let it happen to the cake, it would break her heart. There had to be a way.

A diversion. She pushed over a barrel and crept closer to the opening. Good! The workers ran over to the upturned barrel.

70

"Oh nooo!" she screamed. The cake! Her cake was rolling toward the opening. She saw the seagulls waiting. Althea couldn't tolerate the loss . . . she lunged.

A TRANSVESTITE REQUESTS...

Claire L. Brown

Restaurants could use a third toilet
To cope with cross dressers like me,
Who can't decide which room to use,
Yet, understandably, still must wee.

The challenge occurs while out dining;
Comes time to use the loo.
Gentlemen won't allow me in theirs,
But then, who would? Would you?

Women can't tell I'm a man
Unless they glance under the door
To see my feet facing the bowl,
A scene they greatly abhor.

I get a kick wearing girlish dresses
With legs shaved neath' sheer hose.
When I strut with a feminine wiggle,
Seemingly, no one knows.

My wife longs for a third toilet
When I don my frilly clothes.
She hardly can bear to watch me
Paint my nails or blot my nose.

She snaps, "You really shouldn't be in here!"
But where am I to go?
Would you relegate me to an outdoor bush?
I'd be arrested soon, you know.

A third toilet would please us odd ones.
Congress might consider our plight.
There are enough of us to rate a third room,
And no one would need to take flight.

Is a third toilet too much to ask
In this era of `understanding?'
LADIES, GENTS, and THOSE UNSURE,
Or are we being a bit too demanding?

72

TWILIGHT TIME

Jeanne Freed

Everyone bows their heads in commiseration. "How sad. So tragic," they say. Some truly know these feelings, others silently pray that it never happens to anyone they love.

My father was diagnosed with Alzheimer's disease eight years ago. It is a fatal disease, and eventually he will die but more likely from a different disorder. Modern health care has afforded new options and created new dilemmas. Somewhere along the way, the meaning of right to live and right to die became muddled by the abilities of specialized care facilities. Early treatment can only briefly arrest the steady decline and inevitable complete memory loss. Death with dignity is the quest, but rare is the individual who attains this lofty desire.

I will never forget my father asking me if I'd decorated the tree yet. The occasion was Easter. Since some people have Easter trees, I sincerely hoped that's what he meant. All too soon, there was no way to deny his dementia and the dreaded word "Alzheimer's".

My amazing stepmother struggled valiantly to care for him at home. Her days grew incredibly long, painful, and lonely. She kept constant surveillance to prevent him from wandering away or injuring himself. He no longer knew knives were sharp, or that he couldn't walk through glass. His memory of his wife and children disappeared, randomly making a tormenting reappearance and finally moving permanently into a past we didn't share. We became a composite of his parents, sister, cousins, past loves, and total strangers. It was a daily grind of assurance, nurturing, and constant attention with very little acknowledgement in return.

Sundown brought confusion manifested by screaming, sobbing, and unpredictable violence. His balance was affected, and he began to fall, usually hitting his head against a wall or table. At two hundred and fifty pounds, getting him back on his feet took hours, often requiring emergency assistance. After two years of home care, the time came to find a full care facility.

Within months, his overall health improved, as he was placed on a restricted diet, a passive exercise program, and fortified with nutritional supplements. His body was better, but his mental faculties continued to decline. He couldn't see much, because he swallowed his contact lenses, and flushed three pairs of glasses down the toilet. Since he couldn't read words anymore, eyeglasses were deemed unnecessary.

After a year, he quit talking, and began crying constantly with no related stimulus. The effect was emotional for us, but rationale insisted there were no related feelings behind his tears. He did not know us, could not communicate with us, and had no control of bodily functions. Touching him and talking at him was about all we could do. Every fall, we signed forms allowing vaccination against influenza and pneumonia. Twinges of "why?" became stronger with every passing year.

During the first three years in the residence, his only medical problems were irritated hemorrhoids, stomach flu, and temporary facial drooping from Bell's palsy. Another year passed with moderate, almost imperceptible decline. Then his partial plate went the same way as his eyeglasses, and his remaining teeth began to break off at the gumline. The dentist did not advise putting him through the strains of replacing teeth. Solid food was replaced with spoon fed pureed.

I always felt the worst possible scenario would be for our love to be twisted into feelings of disgust or worse still, indifference. But with time, the disease took a man of meticulous hygiene and turned him into an infant whose whole source of amusement was his body and its various excrements. Still his vital organs remain viable. Ironically, when asked about his health, all we can reply is, "He's fine."

His last physical check up showed his blood pressure elevated indicating signs of potential stroke. We were advised to medicate him with a stroke inhibitor. If I thought for one second he would wake up tomorrow, smile, and say hello, I would do anything for him. But under these circumstances, if a stroke were possible, who with a shred of sanity would try to stop it?

We chose not to medicate. A week later, a nurse said he seemed "perkier" and they were going to begin speech therapy.

The legal papers we'd instituted denied extreme rescue measures and included a "do not recessitate" order. We lost the man we loved many years ago, but still we cannot completely grieve. Our "progress" in the world of modern medicine, will leave a legacy without a conclusion.

Have we gone too far... or perhaps not done enough?

CHANGE OF HEART
Claire L. Brown

Clara slumped down in her chair on the balcony, tears welling in her eyes. Too much had gone wrong lately. Now she was left alone with emptiness, no appetite, a headache, and a feeling that the world had collapsed around her.

She watched drifting clouds thicken off in the distance. A slight breeze suddenly grew into a strong wind. She didn't move. "The storm within me is far worse than the one approaching," she sighed heavily. "I suppose friends would say I'm feeling sorry for myself. Well, I am. I don't care if I live or die." Her eyes closed as she shut out her surroundings.

The ring of the doorbell broke the spell. Quickly collecting herself, she was surprised to see one of the little girls from another apartment at her screen door. Looking up at Clara with a proud smile, she announced, "Its May Day, and I've brought you a basket of treats and things that I made all by myself." She was bouncing with enthusiasm.

When Clara thanked her and invited her in for juice and cookies, the child was inside before the sentence was finished, then asked in a pleadingly polite voice if they could PULEESE eat their treats out on the balcony.

"I see you up here lots of times, and I always wonder about all the things you can see that we can't see from down below. You know, you could even be a spy if you wanted to," she said with a giggle.

Clara began pointing out various things visible from her higher vantage point three stories up, such as birds building nests, squirrels chasing each other along tree branches, woodpeckers pecking out morning wake up calls, new spring buds popping out, stray pets sniffing along sidewalks, and delivery men making their rounds.

"Probably, my favorite thing," she continued, "is to watch the complete turmoil of birds and animals when an owl swoops down into a tree top. I am never sure if the squawks and scrambling are from fear of the owl, or just general excitement and commotion; it's a fascinating mystery."

Suddenly, a voice called out, "Kristin, Kristin!"

"Oh, that's my Mom. Yoo hoo, Mom! I'm way up here on the balcony having cookies with my new friend. She has her own pet owl that I can come and see any time I want to."

Off Kristin ran, dropping the May basket in a chair on her way out, as jelly beans tumbled across the floor.

Clara had to chuckle, not recalling that she had claimed to have an owl as a pet, or that she actually had invited Kristin to pay a return visit to see it; however, she found herself excited over the thought that little Kristin wanted to come back, basket or no basket, owl or no owl. She decided to make a batch of chocolate chip cookies, knowing how much kids love them.

JOHNNY

Jeanne Freed

Death seemed inevitable and unavoidable. Still, I was ill prepared. The grieving process was compounded by confusion. Who was I grieving for? Two people died that day in March of 1988. One was a forty two year old man who suffered the torture of many years diseased by paranoid schizophrenia. The other was a youth, filled with love and hope for the future. The man was John, and the boy was Johnny, and they were both my brother.

On the surface, it was simple; a sister's love for her brother. A lifetime joined with intimate knowledge of one another. But ours was not a simple relationship. We had known great love and intense hate.

There was no easy, rational way to sum up our past. My memories of my brother conjured two images, like a split screen. On one side, he was smiling, his eyes clear and loving . . .forever young. On the other side appeared a tormented visage, mouth curled in sinister sneer, eyes serpentine and taunting, This second image was infinitely more frightening.

Though snapshots from our childhood are now yellowed and brittle, they reveal a past I can never deny. Every picture of me includes my brother, usually with his arm locked about me in a protective embrace. To remember that boy in the pictures, I had to sweep away the debris of more potent images.

As I look back, I can only imagine I was incredibly naive or simply the progeny of old family values. My parents never discussed problems or concerns in front of their children. We apparently were to remain blissfully unaware of life's challenges until we faced them as adults. Though John was often difficult or moody, I never questioned his emotions or personality. He was just being Johnny.

Then came the time of the Vietnam War. John was fresh out of high school, hoping to be accepted at the Chicago Art Institute for second semester. Unfortunately, he got a low draft number instead. To avoid the army, he enlisted in the Air Force. He seemed okay with the whole idea, and so did my parents. But I was only fourteen, starting high school, with no understanding of the military or the ramifications of war. I just missed my brother.

After boot camp, he was sent to Wyoming and assigned to the motor pool. He seemed in no danger of being sent to Asia. After about a year in the service, he started being switched to different assignments every couple of weeks, everything from mess hall to teaching pottery to officers wives. Through letters and phone calls, I got the impression that he wasn't concerned and found his duties rather amusing. But after a couple of months he was transferred to Fitzsimmon's Hospital in Denver for observation. My parents told me it was probably nothing. Knowing John's intellect, and his ability to outsmart most people, I assumed he'd figured out a way to trick the military and get a discharge. After six months in Denver, he was discharged and sent home.

I found out quickly how wrong my assumption was. A man came home who looked like Johnny, but was a complete stranger. At any given moment, he could be laughing hysterically over a private entertainment, or unleash a furious diatribe. His anger was senseless and enraged, usually based on an imagined affront.

The new John was devious and perverse, responding only to the voices he heard in his head. Sometimes his diversions were directed at me. I will never forget the day my little cat, Tigger, disappeared. She always met me at the door when I came home from school, but that day she was nowhere to be found John lurked behind me as I searched and called for her, a smug look of amusement contorting his face. The realization that he was responsible was nearly incomprehensible. But suddenly, I just knew.

Though nearly hysterical, I tried desperately to appeal to any sense of compassion he had left. He didn't deny my accusation. His eyes turned steely with a look of complete contempt. In a cold voice, he said the cat was evil and had been taken care of.

Days later, he groveled before me, pawing at my legs and begging me to forgive him. His face was a mask of terror, and for a few moments I glimpsed the contorted workings of his mind. He could not understand himself, why he had done what he had done. Still, he would not tell me what happened to Tigger. The bond we had was irretrievably broken; and I never trusted him again.

Though we sought professional help for John, and he often admitted himself to the psychiatric ward, laws and insurance allowed only temporary respite before quick release arrived with a new prescription for Thorazine. At that time, drug treatment was simply a different kind of hell. Incapable of any rational thought, John moved in slow motion with vacant disinterest. In some ways, treatment was more heartbreaking than letting the illness run its course.

The power he held over our family was devastating. Every day was filled with tension and overwhelming stress. No one could control him. His insanity gave him the freedom to terrorize anyone in his path Thinking it would keep him from endangering anybody else, my parents took his car away from him. Our home became the battle zone. I couldn't have any friends over, nor was my bedroom a safe haven. Often I would awaken in the morning to see him standing over me, with a grin on his face and a diabolical glint in his eyes. Sometimes he would walk away, and other times, he would wait until I couldn't take it anymore and fled from the room. He seemed to thrive on this form of mental defilement.

I was the only one who could escape the hell John had created. As soon as I finished high school I moved away. My parents wanted someone to survive and I left with their blessing and hope, though my guilt was immense. My logical side knew I could not be my brother's keeper, because eventually I would join him in the depths of humanity, my future extinguished by his. I created a new life, something John would never be able to do. I went home only one more time, when my mother lay dying.

Her physician and hospital security had banned John from seeing her. He had physically attacked our mother and created what was described as an "obscene commotion". I was secretly glad, because it allowed me to be with her and not have to deal with him. But at night, away from the hospital, I watched him closely hoping to see compassion or grief or any hint of feeling. He appeared unconcerned, never asking about Mom, blithely doing whatever he felt like, and ignoring the emotions surrounding the rest of us.

We insisted he go to the funeral believing we'd forever regret his absence, and hoping he would finally grieve for her. Instead, he turned an already heartbreaking experience into an ethereal hell. John was defiant and refused to show any respect for our mother. Instead he forced his way in front of the casket, smiling broadly and swinging his arms wildly as though he were at a parade . At the cemetery, he decided to giggle as the casket was lowered into the ground.

For the next fifteen years, even though I saw him occasionally, he existed in the furthest periphery of my life. I couldn't hate him, because I knew it was the schizophrenia. But I didn't really love him either. I always regretted that there was never a chance to say goodbye to Johnny, he disappeared before I realized he was gone. But passing time has allowed me to remember.

Johnny once found an abandoned kitten in a field near our house. For days he cradled the tiny creature in a warm towel, patiently feeding it milk from an eyedropper and gently stroking its fur. When the kitten was strong and healthy, he scoured the neighborhood until he found it a good home.

One summer in Wisconsin, he good naturedly instructed me how to jig for sunfish, even though I adamantly refused to touch the worm. He taught me to drive a stick shift and never laughed when I stalled the engine. A wonderful artist, he once delighted me with a pencil sketch of all four Beatles. Johnny always cuddled next to me, as Mom read aloud about the "great gray greasy Limpopo River" in "The Elephant's Child" or the Emerald City in "The Wizard of Oz". These were the memories to be cherished.

Though it has taken far too long, I can at last admit how much I loved my brother, and know that he loved me. I'm certain that he loved our mother, and his actions were beyond his control. There is nothing to forgive anymore.

He no longer hears the voices in his head and rests in peace at last.

CAN'T HELP IT

Claire L. Brown

Alcoholics can't help it
Gamblers can't help it
Smokers can't help it
Transvestites can't help it
Bi-sexuals can't help it
Kleptomaniacs can't help it
Xenophobics can't help it
Pyromaniacs can't help it
Sadists can't help it
Masochists can't help it
Drug addicts can't help it
Misogynists can't help it
Road ragers can't help it
Child abusers can't help it
Ad infinitum.

By the year 2050, will there be a need any longer for the word, "responsibility" in the English dictionary?

DONKEY SERENADE

NO SLEEP

A jackass found himself in a plight,
But his bray was worse than his bite.
He screeched for help,
A most terrible yelp,
Hee-hawing all through the night

Claire L. Brown

PRAIRIE PATTERNS*

Shirley Meier

Recently I visited western North Dakota where I grew up and was happy to see many old friends and places, but part of my quest was to also see some spirits of the past. This led me to the country cemetery near Glen Ullin, where my maternal grandparents, Karl and Katherine Kreis, are buried. As newly married German Russian immigrants, they came to that area a hundred years ago, homesteading the land and raising their family.

Late one afternoon, I left Interstate 94 and traveled along the old Highway 10 through the Curlew Valley to a place called Eagle's Nest. There was no evidence of the former railroad stop and only those who recognize the location will know where to turn off the paved road. Even I had to look closely at the scoria covered side road to make sure I was on the right path.

The tracks were still there and while no passenger train service serves the area any more, I was greeted by a low whistle from a locomotive, pulling an endless chain of cars loaded with coal from Montana. The cargo was headed east for Duluth where it will be loaded on ships bound for Europe. How different than in former days when the railroad was the lifeline of this area, bringing westward the settlers from foreign countries. It also brought them the necessities of their new life, such as plows, lumber, tools, food stuffs, household goods, and mail. Later their harvested grain and cattle were shipped back to market on those rails.

On the side of the road stood several large cottonwood trees, now part of a large pasture. A long fence line and orderly, cultivated fields lay beyond but no other visible landmarks were to be seen. The structures here had long ago been demolished but this was the place where my parents lived when I was born. I opened the car window and the smell of the prairie grass engulfed me. As I took a big breath, I felt the ghosts of the past hover around me in a solid place of my memory. But there was no need to get out, I told myself, for it was all gone. But I did so anyway and climbed through the fence.

To the side was a hill and beyond buttes rose to enclose the valley. It was very quiet, as only the remote prairie can be, but suddenly a gentle breeze moved through the trees making the leaves sing. Perhaps as an infant I heard that same lullaby of nature, held by Mother on the porch shaded by these very trees. We know so little of our beginnings,

I mused, gazing across the gray green pasture land to a rippling field of golden wheat.

In the far distance once stood the old home place, the homestead of my grandparents. The last time I saw it was thirty years ago when my husband, two daughters and I took the road that skirted the nearby hill. There before us stood the red barn, white bungalow, outhouse and sheds. It looked like countless other rural American farmyards but this one was different because it was the symbol of my personal heritage. Here my mother grew up and met my father. I remember coming many times as a child, visiting my aunt and uncle who owned the place in later years.

But that visit was to be my last one. My relatives were retiring and moving to town. Though the land would still be farmed, the house was to be moved off the property, the barn taken apart and the other buildings torn down or removed. The windmill was already gone, replaced by an electric pump, and the corral and fencing were to be changed to house range cattle.

Looking at the overgrown road to the site now, I realized that it wasn't a good idea to drive there. Long gone were the days when the children skipped barefoot along the dusty ruts. Here it was that my youngest uncle, as a child, wandered away from home and getting tired, took a nap in the high grass nearby. He wasn't found for hours and only then did the tiny footprints lead the family to him.

Getting back in the car, I looked up and down the graveled road. I couldn't help wondering how my Kreis grandparents felt the first time they came this way. It was, of course, then only a primitive dirt trail and though later it basically followed the section lines, in the early days they probably took a few shortcuts over the virgin prairie. Even so, it was an eight mile trip by horse and wagon from town.

Having arrived by train from the eastern part of the state where they had wintered after arriving in America from Southern Russia, they saw Glen Ullin, an already established town several years old. It boasted three general stores, livery stables, equipment shops, churches, bars, a school and private homes. But the buildings were still standing quite naked along the railroad tracks and the Big Muddy Creek which formed the base of the valley.

There they loaded their few personal belongings and the equipment that they brought into a purchased wagon and team. Two bellowing milk cows were tied to the back as they moved slowly down the dusty street toward the edge of town and I'm sure, the edge of anticipation and fear. Soon they were traveling along the lonely grassy trail with the limitless sky above them. They certainly thought about the challenge of their new circumstances. Only later, as winter came, would they fully realize the true isolation of their new lives.

From their train ride, my grandparents had seen that the towns of the Great Plains were miles and miles apart and that the soil didn't support the lush growth of their expectation. In Europe they had always lived in small villages with close neighbors, farming the nearby land. They could often see the neighboring town but on this prairie, there was only the far away horizon. Because of the distance, it was obvious to them that to utilize the land, people had to actually live on it. In fact, the Homestead Act required them to stay for five years in order to stake the 160 acre claim. If they planted trees, they could obtain another 160 acres.

They probably didn't think about the area's original citizens, but they shared many things in common with the Mandan, who had grown corn on the banks of the Missouri or the wandering Sioux who chased buffalo over the prairie. They too would be tied to the earth for their existence as well. Like their ancestors in South Russia a hundred years ago who developed the land vacated by the departing Turks around the Black Sea, so they now had to tame this frontier. The toil of breaking sod, planting, herding cattle and harvesting wasn't easy. When the rains came, it was welcome, but the drought, the heat and the grasshoppers also had to be endured.

I looked down the road to another invisible place where the one room country school once stood. Here the children of immigrants rode their ponies to lessons in English, mathematics, and government. Though the valley was settled with many from the Old Country and my grandparents had comfort in that bond, the next generation became different. They had a new language and a different approach but when drought and depression of the 1930's hit, many of them left for the West Coast where there was hope of work. Those who remained in North Dakota struggled until rain fell and prices rose during the next two decades. However, they also saw their children lured far away to better jobs, repeating the pattern of many before them. I know, for I was one of them.

Since it was getting late, I drove down the road. Soon a small fenced area with a wrought iron gate emerged out of the grass. The white country church, a proud landmark seen for miles, had once stood on the adjoining rise. Here was the heart of their community, the place to sing and worship, to meet neighbors, to share lunch baskets after church. A few hitching posts still remained, a reminder for those passing by in air conditioned cars that often teams of horses, gently switching their tails at flies and munching on the grass, waited here for the ranchers and farmers to finish their worship.

There were several dozen graves. The Germanic names on the markers were a roll call of my earliest memories. The headstones still stood erect and the plots outlined with small rocks looked fairly tidy but there hadn't been much recent activity. Big sunflowers swayed against the fence. I read the weathered names of my grandparents and moved to the two tiny markers of infants lost to them nearly a century ago. An uncle was also buried nearby. I felt the mourning ghosts standing around the fresh graves. Brushing my hand against the headstones, I tearfully turned away.

The sun was about to set; I needed to leave. I looked toward the fields and heard the mooing of cows as a herd appeared over a ridge. They stopped, both surprised and curious about what they saw. What was I doing there? I asked the same question. Why did I come and what had I discovered in my step back in time?

The answer was simple. I'd come to honor my heritage. Though the buildings hadn't survived, I saw that the enriched landscape was a proud testimony to the efforts of the early settlers. I cherished the values about their reverence for God, the bonds of family, stewardship of the land, the dignity of hard work and the courage to be a pioneer in a strange land. Though my personal ancestors had passed away, their pattern, their imprint was upon me. They would understand me, for they too traveled far from home to have a new life.

The few local descendants remaining have become the proud old families. They follow familiar footsteps but for the rest of us who are scattered, we only have the luxury of occasionally visiting. But unlike our grandparents from Russia and their German grandparents before them who never had the option of returning to the land of their birth, we can still feel the prairie breeze on our faces, gaze over the wide horizon, and know this is where they lived and this land is our heritage.

*PRAIRIE PATTERNS appeared in the JOURNAL OF THE AMERICAN HISTORICAL SOCIETY of Germans from Russia in 2001.

SOMEBODY'S LITTLE PUMPKIN

Jeanne Freed

After an appendectomy, I took advantage of electronic communication, and emailed a blanket statement to everybody in my address book. Among the recipients was Kathleen, my first cousin once removed (my mother's first cousin). She is the last surviving member of that generation of my kin, and fortunately she has accepted computers and enjoys corresponding by email.

Her reply was newsy and spoke at length about her husband's ordeal with his appendectomy twenty years before. Fortunately for me, the surgery is now done laparoscopically, and I was not going to be subjected to the same type of recovery. Her correspondence ended by saying, "So heal well my little pumpkin, Love Kathleen".

I couldn't believe it when I saw the words "my little pumpkin", and smiled that she still thought of me as a little girl. But then it hit me that I hadn't been called a little pumpkin by anybody since my mother died when I was twenty one. I've been missing something for so long, I didn't even remember I missed it. My mother died thirty years ago and I've missed her every day since, but I have memories to sustain me. Of course, there have been thousands of moments I longed to have her with me, to share a hug, a smile, advice or approval. Still, I was floored to realize I missed something tiny, seemingly insignificant, but so precious. For over thirty years, I haven't been anybody's baby girl. I have been my husband's sweetie, but I have never been his "baby". I have friends and children, and a full life, but I haven't been a little pumpkin and forgot that I ever was.

My daughters have been my pumpkins, and my sweetpeas, and the endearments always came easily and often. I'm certain they never even think about it, as I know I never did. They are just words that mothers call their children without a second thought. I never knew how much I missed those little words, but remembering that she called me "my little pumpkin" was a special and unexpected gift.

Thanks Kathleen.

AWAY FROM / WITH PROGRESS
Claire L. Brown

Is progress the answer to quality of life,
Where changes sing the "rat race" song?
Often we need a different venue
Away from crowds and milling throng.

Great distance isn't required
To wander off on greener sod
To tranquil hide-aways nearby
Where hang the very skirts of God.

We seek places to ponder or celebrate,
Places which progress overlooks;
Places where we can be alone
With clovered fields and babbling brooks.

Technology crammed in skyscrapers
Encroaches on nature, causing harm,
Encouraging us to seek respite
In places of idyllic charm.

We long to find an inn where we might linger
Away from noisy clamor and voices brusque,
To sit back in leisure, and gaze upon
The rose embroidered cloth of dusk.

Early morning dew on parking lots
Offers no verdant Shang-ri-la.
We must speak up. Now is the hour.
Transitions go quickly from meadow to mall.

DREAM A LITTLE DREAM

Jeanne Freed

This wasn't right. It couldn't be right! But how could he deny what his eyes were seeing? Darlene was ripping the ears off Molly's favorite stuffed bunny. She was smiling and muttering, "She'll never forget to make her bed again!"

Darlene was a kind and loving mother. Why was she being so cruel?

Molly would be heartbroken; she loved BunBun more than anything. The little girl never went anywhere without the pink rabbit, and the family always included BunBun in their adventures, often treating the bunny like a person. Darlene and Molly had a standing appointment to bathe BunBun once a month. Together they laughed and talked while fluffing the bunny's tail and ears. The event always ended with tying a crisp new bow around BunBun's neck.

He wanted to stop her but felt removed, like an observer with no voice, confused, perplexed and more than a little frightened. This could not be his wife.

A bleating sound rang in his ears. It wouldn't stop. His brow furrowed, and his eyes fluttered. A thin streak of sun met his eyes.

"Good morning. You sure were restless, did you have a bad dream?"

The voice. It was Darlene. A dream? Was it a dream? Of course, his waking mind confirmed, it was only a dream. Stretching, he let out a welcome prolonged yawn. Throwing his arms around his wife, he gave her a resounding kiss on the top of her head. "Yeah, I had a lousy dream, but it didn't make a lick of sense. I'm gonna hit the shower." Bounding out of bed, he hurried toward the bathroom. Darlene always wanted to hear about his dreams, but he wasn't about to share this one. Still it bothered him. He remembered the look on her face in the dream... strangely different, almost evil.

Downstairs, Chili, the family dog, heartily greeted him. A few hearty pats on the head later, his attention drew to his daughters sitting at the table eating cold cereal. BunBun sat next to Molly's bowl in her usual spot. The stuffed rabbit's ears were somewhat askew, but firmly attached. It was just a dumb dream, not worth thinking about.

He'd been dreading going to the dump. The landfill was over an hour's drive north. But they had so much junk piling up in the back yard the trip was necessary.

"I can hardly move with all these boxes crushed up against my knees, Daddy."

"I know Sweetpea, but . . ."

"It's too crowded in here. Pull over."

He didn't know why, but did as Darlene said.

"Get out Debbie. We'll pick you upon the way back."

What? No . . . This was a terrible section of town. Drug pushers crouched in every storefront. Why were they leaving Debbie here alone?

Debbie climbed over her sister and mother, slowly setting one foot then the other on the sidewalk. His firstborn daughter looked so tiny in her thin blue jacket, with her blond hair fluttering in the breeze, and little face pale with terror. Still he was driving away, leaving his child, because Darlene told him to.

He drove like a maniac. Wildly, he pitched everything from the truck bed and raced back to the place they left Debbie. She was gone. A scream welled in his throat. He felt like he was being eviscerated. DEBBIEEEEE. . .

"Wake up honey! You're having a nightmare."

Her hand was on his shoulder. How could she touch him after what she'd done? He lashed out and pushed Darlene away. His rage was overwhelming. The hatred he felt was like a fire blazing behind his eyes.

"Calm down Honey. It's okay, it was just a bad dream."

He looked at her closely. Her eyes were puffy with sleep, dark hair tangled and messy. Still, she looked concerned. The small lines around her mouth held his attention. They were smile lines. Darlene always smiled.

But she was evil! Look what she'd done to their daughters. Or did she? He muttered he was sorry and again, ran for the shower.

The dreams became more vivid each night, the intensity staying with him throughout the day. On Saturday, when he could have slept in, the horror of Darlene's latest deed woke him hot and trembling. Seeing Chili stretched out with his paws crossed did nothing to alleviate the vision of his wife punishing the dog with an electric knife for tracking mud on her clean floor.

Darlene sat at the kitchen table perusing the newspaper and munching down the last bits of her toast. Smiling, she turned her cheek towards him expecting a morning kiss. Mustering his severely depleted strength, he pursed dry lips and pressed them to the side of her head.

"You missed," she giggled.Rising from her chair, Darlene planted her mouth on his lips.

He pulled away, instantly disgusted and nauseous. The lingering sweet smell of orange marmalade on her breath made him want to vomit. Heat rose to his face, and he swallowed the bile collecting in his throat

"What was that look for?" Darlene was staring at him with eyes moist and round.

The hurt he saw on her face suddenly made him want to laugh. Who was she to act wounded after the horrific things she'd done? But he was bewildered. She looked so sweet and innocent, just like the day they married. Flashes of memories reminded him of their many joys. Still, she was in his dreams . . . the other Darlene... the one he hated

"I'm sorry," he managed. "I just haven't been sleeping well, and...and...I don't know."

Immediately Darlene's hurt disappeared and her voice became soothing and concerned. "It's those nightmares isn't it? Why won't you talk about them, maybe I can help."

"I don't want to talk about them," he shouted. "I don't even want to think about them. And if I did, you'd be the last person I'd talk to, you bitch." Struggling to control his anger, he could hear his last words echo through the kitchen.

Darlene looked like she'd been slapped Did he slap her? He couldn't remember. He wanted to...

"Mommy?" Molly's sleepy face peered from around the corner.

Darlene rushed to their daughter, clinging to the child as if protecting her. "Good morning Baby . . .did Mommy and Daddy wake you?"

"I heard yelling and Daddy said a bad word"

He couldn't believe what he was seeing. Darlene was being all saintly and soothing Molly while he stood being accused of some misdeed. It was absurd; he was the one who protected his children. But he had to admit he wasn't doing a very good job. Look at all the things he'd let happen "Come here Molly," he said with urgency. He had to get her away from that woman.

Instead, Molly snuggled closer to her mother. "Baby, why don't you run upstairs and go potty and brush your teeth. Daddy didn't mean to say a bad word, he just," Darlene glared at him, "stubbed his big toe and got an owie."

He was incensed. She was lying and that was against the rules. He watched his daughter head back up the stairs as Darlene slowly rose and turned to face him. Her face was pale but her eyes were dark and determined. "What is wrong?" she asked quietly.

He found himself backing up a couple of steps, at first afraid, then slowly realizing she meant her words. Her concern was unfeigned and genuine, and she was scared. Though the kitchen was chilled with early fall coolness, he was flushed with perspiration. Reaching the sink he turned the cold water faucet on full blast. Instead of opting for a few splashes, he immersed his whole head under the icy flow. Without drying off, he turned letting rivulets of water drip down his neck. Wide eyed, he saw Darlene standing a few feet away, wearing her worn fleecy robe and twisting nervous fingers around her dangling belt. He saw their dog standing next to her staring at him, with ears at attention. He smelled the coffee in the pot, and finally saw everything was like it always was. "I'm okay now."

"No, you're not okay. What are these dreams about?"

With all his being, he did not want to tell her but he was out of control. His dreams and reality were all mixed up. "They seem to be about you, only it isn't you. In my dreams you have an evil twin."

"Excuse me?"

Smiling wanly he continued, explaining without the gory details and perhaps sugar coating some of the more heinous events.

Darlene stared at him fascinated by his imagination. "Why do you suppose all of a sudden you're dreaming like this every night? Did I do something or has something changed?"

"Believe me I've racked my brain trying to come up with a reason. It's like my subconscious takes over the instant I fall asleep. I know you but the person you are when I'm asleep is someone I don't know."

"I think you need to see a doctor. Maybe hypnosis or whatever they do can explain all this. We can't go on like this, I was really afraid of you."

Though it still seemed strangely distasteful, he placed his arm around her and pulled her close. "I'm sorry I scared you. Know anybody else who's crazy and has a good shrink?"

He couldn't see their family physician until Monday afternoon... two more days and worse yet, two more nights. Hoping the change would help, he told Darlene he would spend the night on the couch in the family room. He left the television on flipping between a comedy and a Japanese monster flick, hoping the banality would somehow switch off the need to dream.

They were sitting around the picnic table, the aroma of sizzling burgers wafting in the summer breeze. Debbie unloaded a heavy tray of dishes and silverware, meticulously placing plates and utensils and lining up the napkins with a ruler. Her face was flushed and her hands trembled with each movement. Little Molly stepped through the patio door balancing a large pitcher and four cut crystal goblets. He began to step toward her to help but Darlene's hand stopped him.

"Let's see if she passes the test," she insisted.

At the sound of Darlene's voice, Molly stumbled and the pitcher rocked precariously on the tray. When it seemed to right itself, a goblet tumbled hitting the next one and creating a slow motion domino effect. The glass shattered against the concrete patio and lemonade splashed his shoes.

"You know what to do now don't you, little miss."

Wanting desperately to help he rushed quickly into the house for a dustpan and broom. Expecting to see Molly working on the mess he was startled to see her raising the lid on the gas grill. With Darlene hovering over her, Molly brought her hands down over the open flame.

This time he awoke crying.

Somehow he stifled the rage rippling through his body. Instead he kept busy with household chores, distancing himself from his wife and daughters. When night came began drinking coffee and refused the urge to sleep.

After thirty six hours of with no sleep, his words flowed with a keen edge of desperation. The doctor listened solicitously, but believed it was only stress and prescribed strong sleeping pills. When the medication didn't work the first two nights, he doubled the dosage, and still the dreams didn't stop. The pills only made his role in the scenarios even less effectual than before.

Hostility for his wife affected every waking moment, his thoughts were of nothing but the dreams. A simple "Hi, how are you?" would launch him into a diatribe about his marriage that assuredly made no sense to the listener. He began showing up late for work nearly every day and co workers began to distance themselves from him. He was jeopardizing his job, but it seemed inconsequential compared to his nightly torture. Colleagues whispering about him seemed a mere annoyance rather than a cause for concern. When lifelong friends began forgetting to tell him about the next poker night, he noticed but couldn't seem to really care. But when Debbie told him she was getting too big for him to tuck her in at night, and Molly pretended to already be asleep, he was deeply hurt. His torment was for his daughters but they didn't know it. He was alone, unable to save his children from their mother.

He called his doctor several times a day ranting and pleading for relief. There had to be something that would shut his mind off and stop this agony. At first, the doctor droned on with psychobabble about daytime stresses festering in the subconscious. An odyssey began as he went from one therapist to another with no answers. He tried stress management workshops, biofeedback, Chinese herbs, meditation, aromatherapy, sound recordings of raindrops, and a ridiculous visit with a past life progression counselor. The dreams intensified, becoming more extreme in nature. His quest only produced a theme of avoiding sugar, saturated fats and caffeine, and a notion that he'd once been a buccaneer in the Caribbean. His regular doctor finally prescribed a "revolutionary" psychotropic drug complete with a journal for recording his reaction. He only made one notation before he nearly bludgeoned Darlene to death.

He neither saw nor heard from Darlene or his daughters. His attorney did tell him that Darlene was recovering and she and the children were staying with her parents. The next three months were spent in the county jail as he awaited trial. There had been no dreams of any kind since the morning of his brutal attack on his wife. Strangely, he slept better than he ever remembered.

Darlene looked fragile and thin as she sat at the witness stand and denied any involvement in the alleged attack. Innocently, she claimed it was unprovoked and that her husband of nine years was a madman entirely capable of murder. He wanted to take the stand and tell the jury that she was the demented one, constantly devising unspeakable punishment, but his appointed attorney was hoping for an insanity plea. He kept telling anyone who'd listen to just look at his daughters and they would know the truth about Darlene. But everyone only shook their heads and told him there were no injuries and the girls were fine.

He was moved to a state mental hospital. At night, the screams and banging from the other cells reminded him of the primate habitat at the zoo but he slept peacefully. Dreams returned but they were pastoral and serene. He was watching autumn leaves dance through the air dropping into a shallow brook and drifting along like little boats...

"Wake up Daddy. Wake up!"

His eyes sang open and tried to focus on the tousle headed child just inches from his face. It was Molly! His heart leapt with joy and amazement. His hands reached out to pull her close. Then he saw her face was crumpled and blotchy with tears streaming down her cheek. "What's wrong Sweetpea?"

"Look what happened!" she sobbed, holding out both hands.

In one hand she clutched her well loved BunBun. In the other hand were two little pink fuzzy ears.

BESTEMOR'S BEST

Claire L. Brown

My bestemor (grandmother, in Norwegian) slipped practical advice into our chats along with a krumkake cookie, a cup of strong egg coffee, and a broad smile. I never felt she was preaching, and always wanted to hear more. Often she shared a story from her past to illustrate what she wanted to say. Here are some of her bits of wisdom:

1. Turn trouble into a memorable or learning experience. For instance, when your electricity goes out during a storm, light candles, and roast hot dogs over a fire. You might even tell ghost stories. The electricity will be restored in the same amount of time no matter what you do.

2. Sit toward the front of your classes. Those who want to show they aren't interested always head for the back row. One day, while teaching a history class, Bestemor surprised her students by having everyone move back one row; she then requested those in the very back to move up to the front.

3. Be a pleasure to have around. When invited to a friend's house for dinner, offer to help set or clear the table. Even if your help is not needed, the mother will always remember that you offered.

4. Your table manners should be impeccable, never fooling with your hair, fingernails, or food remnants caught in your teeth. Keep elbows and purses off the table. Gentlemen always remove hats, and refrain from tilting back chairs. Trying to be tactful, one day she quipped, "A couple of your friends are potential gentlemen; they just haven't caught on yet. One thing nice concerning good table manners is that they are free and available to everyone, rich or poor."

5. Don't speak extra loudly in everyday conversation, or scream for no good reason. Speak in the same key as those around you. It's surprising how a few people seem to remain unaware. In a restaurant, for instance, haven't we all had to listen to a diner at another table whose off pitched loud voice penetrated the entire room?

6. To make a point, avoid yelling. To teach a lesson, avoid yelling. Even when training an animal, avoid yelling. Louder isn't better; in fact, it is usually far less effective.

7. Never sign your name to anything you're not proud of. It's bound to show up again sooner or later to give you regrets.

8. Use caution in sharing personal secrets. They all too often get passed on, even by best friends in a weak or non thinking moment.

9. When a friend is sad or suffering, acknowledge their suffering.

Let them know you care no matter how uncomfortable you feel under the circumstances. If you can't think of words beyond, "I'm sorry," an arm around the shoulder will do. Saying things such as, "It could be worse," or "It's God's will," doesn't help.

10. Don't enter a game you can't bear to lose. When and if you do lose, don't offer an excuse such as, "I actually was too tired to play to begin with," or, "I haven't played this game for over a year." It takes the wind out of your opponent's sails. Instead, cheerfully congratulate the winner.

11. Pay more attention to what people do than to what they say. That's the same as saying, "actions speak louder than words." Bestemor once made a prison visit , and found the prisoners quite friendly and fairly well spoken. She had to remind herself as to why they were there. Many had committed atrocious crimes, including murder and serial rape.

12. If you sit around waiting for good things to happen, they may never occur. Help them happen. Bestemor would never listen to me complain about being bored. "Boredom," she said, "implies you lack the creativity and initiative to invent something to do.

13. Count your change when making a purchase. It doesn't mean you're suspicious. Its simply business-like. Go by your instincts in social situations. If a person or situation seems haywire or strangely uncomfortable, leave.

14. Avoid drawing attention to something a person can't change, such as a scar, limp, or deformity of any kind. The time to speak up is when a lady's slip is showing, or a label is hanging out ....things one would want to know, and can correct immediately.

15. Be patient. There always will be those who talk, read, walk, or drive more slowly than you prefer.

16. If you dislike a job for which you have been hired, do your best work right up until you quit, and then quit graciously. You never know when you may want a `good word' from your former employer for a future job. Never quit one job until you have found another. Being without income is no fun.

17. There is no need to be afraid of the dark. Darkness is the same as daylight; its simply darker. With that in mind, my sister and I used to go cross-country skiing in the moonlight, sometimes at midnight.

18. The company you keep will be more fulfilling than the events you attend. Bestemor claimed to have seen endless silly or mediocre movies, but her group of friends always made it worthwhile...or at least fun.

19. Think before complaining about trivial things, such as, "Why

wasn't I born to be taller, or with blonde hair?" The person you are complaining to may have an artificial limb, or worse.

20. Upon receiving a compliment on your attire, no need to quip, "Oh, this old thing. I've had it for years." Be polite enough to just say, "thank you." They really weren't interested in a history of the garment.

21. Avoid wearing an outfit you wouldn't be proud to wear in front of a seminary class, your grandparents or anyone else's for that matter.

22. When dressing casually to go out with friends, make it "smart casual." A rough shirt with sharp jeans or slacks is okay, as is a sharp shirt with rough jeans. However, if you wear a rough shirt with rough jeans or slacks, the total look is dumpy, or unkempt. The latest fad may be a dumpy look, and if that's the case, well ...."de gustibus non est disputandum" (there is no disputing with taste).

23. If someone requires correcting, do it in the kindest possible manner. Announcing, "You're wrong!" won't do. You might say, "I don't think so," or, "There is another point of view we ought to consider here." Try not to allow emotion to eliminate common sense.

24. Show anger if you must, but don't mope. Moping is like wringing your hands or pacing the floor, neither of which accomplishes anything.

25. Whenever a good friend seeks donations for a worthy cause, give, even if you only can give a small amount. That's what friendship is all about.

26. When borrowing something, return more than you borrowed. For instance, if you are loaned a car, return it clean, and full of gas, regardless of the condition it was in when you borrowed it. You might even place a note of thanks on the dash board accompanied by a single rose.

27. Avoid standing in front of or behind a car with the motor running. It could move accidentally. Bestemor had a good friend who was a victim in just such an accident. The car facing her began rolling forward unexpectedly, then ran over her as she slipped when frantically trying to leap out of the way.

28. While performing an odious chore, sing, hum, or whistle. You'll remember the song far longer than the chore.

29. You needn't always require exact answers. There is much Truth without obvious proof or historical accuracy. Santa Claus is an example. He is not an overworked jolly old elf huffing and puffing around the North Pole, but is the `spirit of giving.' We become part of the spirit when we give gifts to others. I remember Bestemor warning, "When you tell me you no longer believe in Santa Claus, then he'll quit coming." I never said it. Ever.

ABOUT GIRLS FROM THE COUNTRY
Shirley Meier

"You can take the girl out of the country..." is the familiar saying that often involved good natured ribbing towards me, a woman with a rural background who has lived in urban America for many years. Though my friends never used the term, "hick from the sticks", I did sense an occasional superiority in their sly smiles when I told them stories about my ranch childhood. However, the unique combination of family, work and nature, bound together by necessity in country living, gave me many positive supports in my life.

The advantage of rural life was that everyone shared a common goal in a common place. Ranching was a private endeavor with little interference from the outside world but we interacted continuously at home. Needing one another and working with one another strengthened those mutual bonds. This scenario defined the core reality and value of family existence in the country. In towns, life had been far more compartmentalized for years (with the possible exception of family shopkeepers) and the growth of modern suburbs added to the separation of families even more because of distance and travel time.

Meanwhile back at the ranch, our whole family was an active part of the operation because my parents seldom had outside help. Agricultural machinery had lessened the grueling physical demands and also the amount of man power needed for much of the ranching jobs, but self sufficiency was still the theme. Business decisions were family affairs and we were flexible with the work load. Generally, my mother did the cooking and baking, while Dad was the mechanic and equipment operator, but we children learned to pitch in almost anywhere. Depending on the situation, Dad washed the dishes and we females milked cows and drove tractors.

A contrast to our lifestyle was made when an older city friend of mine recently announced with pride, "I've never been to my husband's office and he has never done his own laundry." For her, it was a statement of division with dignity, an American Ideal, appropriate to that urban generation, but not to the values of rural people. I didn't share the common experience of city children who never saw their parents working or some who didn't even know where or why they worked.

Another interesting factor had to do with social life. The urban workplace was usually found in public. Although times have now changed, traditionally men tended to work with other men and women spent their days with the children and other neighbor ladies. Their general reason for social events was to mingle with someone of the opposite sex or other couples. Contrarily, in the country, where couples shared their work day, a stronger effort was made to mingle socially with those of one's own gender. How I remember the visits in the fading hours of a summer Sunday, when country women gathered together in the kitchen and men leaned on the corral fences, talking eagerly with one another.

I realized early on that many city born friends of my age and profession held a deeply entrenched concept about the "proper" place of women. As a country female, I had just fallen off the pioneering era and had missed most of the defined feminine one that followed in towns. As a result, I never had to go through the traumatic adjustment about doing "man's work", even if I experienced and resented the differences in pay for women. Separation of rewards in our rural family and an individual's worth were never an issue.

Usually the first questions city friends asked me were about country kids working when they were very young. Some people found it wrong or unacceptable that a girl did things like rake hay or haul bales. They may have thought that my parents should have objected to it. I thought that my tales of milking cows and feeding horses illustrated age appropriate family "chores", not forced labor. The disciplined but not abusive life on our ranch included everyone doing his or her part in various capacities. The simple answer was that if there was a job to be done and if I were able to do it, no other distinctions were made.

Oddly enough, many years later, when my parents retired in town, I saw a vivid example of how gender oriented they had become because of their new location. A small evergreen tree needed transplanting in their yard and I immediately wanted to do it for them. With my rural viewpoint, I didn't consider the fact that it was inappropriate for a woman. Only two reasons registered in my mind as to why I wouldn't do such a task: I hated gardening or I'd have to be very sick. But I was seriously chastised with, "Around here, women don't do that kind of thing." Such a rebuff made me chaff, but my mother understood the stigma of urbanized eyes and mind set better than I .

My sense of imagination was fostered by the rural experience. After the school day, I filled my solitary time as a child with animals and imaginary friends. I played with cattle bones, turning them into animals, trucks or other vehicles in my little behind the garden play area. I used sardine cans for buildings, boats or buggies. I shaped the dirt to form hills and valleys, fields and air strips. Because I didn't have the advantage of neighborhood playmates of my own age, I learned to be self reliant, resourceful and an independent thinker.

I also really enjoyed being with animals and I learned responsibility early in life by caring for them. My understanding went far beyond that of having a fun cuddly playmate. The dogs and cats may have been pets but they also performed a needed function around the ranch. The dogs were used as herding and watch animals while the cats were constantly on mouse patrol in the barns. Again an example of how work and nature were interwoven.

Because we were dependent on nature, we respected it, loved it, and feared it. For children of the country it was more than a place to visit for recreation. We realized that earning a living off the land took wise and careful management. And that didn't come easily. I have enough memories of devastating hailstorms and back aches from hoeing to know Mother Nature was also a tough opponent.

Our environmental philosophy centered on a balanced partnership with the earth, believing that essentially nature was meant to provide for human needs. I valued both the aesthetic views of ravishing sunsets as well as the physical joy of eating fresh corn on the cob. However, it was with slight amusement that we rural women observed the flower children of the 60's trying to return to the land. (We knew many wanted to dodge legal restraint and their main agricultural pursuits were planting pot.) They didn't have the survival skills that were needed and few bothered to acquire any. We understood why they left.

When I moved to the suburbs, I was the one who had to flip directions. Pets became welcoming friends at the end of a busy day. The weekly lawn moving and gardening chores were a therapy from my paper and desk top world. In addition to adding style and charm to my house, those activities prevented the need for a psychologist or an expensive health club membership. It may have served the same function for some of my neighbors, but for me, it was also a ritual of a cherished rural childhood.

Another interesting observation for me in town revolved around sports. Naturally, physical activity keeps one fit but in the country that need wasn't the big draw because we had our exercise built in. Even though we were generally able athletes and appreciated the mental challenge of games, many enjoyed the social and competitive aspects more. We often followed the example of our elders, who after a day or rounding up cattle or fixing fences, preferred a game of cards.

Country people used the principle of "form following function." I did chores in overalls and sturdy shoes but went to dances in dresses and jewelry. Now jeans are the fashion uniforms of contemporary life but years ago, it would have indeed been a country bumpkin who ventured into a social gathering wearing them. It took years of indoctrination to free me (or almost free me) of that double association. Perhaps I should be more grateful that rural influences and savvy designers softened the urban formality.

I appreciate the opportunities that city life gave me, but my greatest regret is that my own children didn't experience a rural childhood. Hopefully, I have shown them the joy of family, the value of work, and the love of nature. For them, they must glean their creative nature from the urban landscape.

But as for me, I'm thankful that they can't ever take the country out of this city girl.

DON'T FENCE ME IN

GIVE IT UP

My jackass entered a race,
But couldn't maintain the pace.
    Though he tried to run fast
    Others whizzed past
His prize was called `last place '

            Claire L. Brown

house. Sure, his dungarees were softer, but they shrunk up in the crotch and barely lasted out a year.

After shutting the gate to the pasture behind him, he moseyed over to the largest of three natural ponds. Toward the end of summer they built up considerable algae often becoming stagnant, depending on the weather. The big pond was still half full. Dark green slime coated the bank on the far side. The pool was murky and brimming with tiny little bugs and microscopic critters. Louis smiled. To him nothing beat the sight of a farm pond fermenting nature's juices.

"This soup isn't bad. Give me another," said Louis with a belch.

"It's probably because I didn't make it," answered Marie, handing him a full bowl. "I picked it up at the deli in town after I saw the doctor."

"He know what's wrong with you?"

"Not really. He took some blood tests, but thought it might be anemia or a bacterial infection. But, he gave me some antibiotics, and I feel a little better."

Louis forgot. She said she was going to the doctor, but it never entered his mind they'd do tests. "What kind of blood tests?"

"I don't know, whatever they do to check for infection or platelets or whatever. Why?"

Damn. Things weren't so high tech twenty years ago. "I just don't want you getting AIDS or something."

"I think that's when you get blood, not give it."

"When is the doctor gonna get back to you?"

"A couple of days."

"Well, I'm sure it's nothing."

A few days later, when Louis came downstairs in the morning, he saw Marie sitting in her rocker bundled up in an old afghan. "You sick again?"

"I feel awful. My stomachs doing the fandango."

"You still taking your medicine?"

"I finished off the last pill five days ago. But I felt fine 'til this morning."

"Well you just rest. I'm going into town for some wire. I can pickup some of that soup like you got at the deli."

"Maybe I should come with you and see if the doctor can take a look at me."

"No!" Louis blurted the word out before he could stop himself. "I mean, you just started feeling poorly, maybe it's just a flu bug, darlin'. See how you feel in a couple of days."

"I guess you're right. Before you leave would you bring up another bottle of that cider you pressed. It came out so tasty, it might make me feel better."

A little smile curled at Louis's lip. "You finished off the first jug already?"

"Yeah, last night."

"Well that's great. Glad you like it. I added some extra spices to it to give it a little heft this year."

Marie smiled wanly. "It's very good Louis." She rose from the chair obviously weak and shaky. "I think I'm going to wander back up to bed Let me know when you get back from town."

"I'll leave the cider in the fridge," Louis said to her retreating back. She mumbled something, but it didn't matter. It was a real stroke of luck that he took the call about the blood test results.

Her voice a whisper, Marie asked, "Did you get a hold of the doctor?"

"I tried, but the phone's out from the storm last night." Marie was so out of it, that she wouldn't even know there was no storm, just a light rain. "I don't want to leave you alone, or I'd drive to town myself." Louis sat on the edge of the bed, patting Marie's thin hand. She looked horrible. Her eyes were like crisp burn holes in a blanket, and her skin was ghostly gray. He didn't remember the first wife ever looking this bad.

"We've got to do something! I feel like I'm dying, Louis." Little pitiful sobs made her sound like a calf stuck in the mud.

"I will, darlin'. You just go on back to sleep while I take care of things." She was out like a light again, her chest moving up and down ever so slightly. Maybe he liked Marie more than he thought. But next time, he was gonna find one good in the kitchen and bedroom. Well anyway, she was practically unconscious, so he might as well see to the stock in the south pasture. No harm in leaving her for a while.

Chores took longer than he expected, and it was nearly sundown when he got back to the house. There were tire tracks in the mud by the steps to the porch. Deep ruts, like somebody took off real fast. Louis felt a sinking feeling in his stomach. The front door was ajar.

Running into the house, taking two steps at a time, he flung open the door to the bedroom. Marie was gone.

The phone rang louder than he'd ever heard. He snatched it from the cradle before the second ring. "Yeah!" he screamed.

"Louis, this is Mona from Dr. Chase's office."

"What have you done with my wife?"

"Calm down Louis! The Doe sent me out to check on her since she missed an appointment. I found her practically in a coma and called an ambulance. She's here at the Medical Center. We've been trying to get a hold of you all day."

"What!" He could feel cold sweat break out across his forehead. "Is she alive?"

"Of course she is. She's in their best room hooked up to an IV. But, she still hasn't regained consciousness. Maybe you should get down here."

"I'll be right there." Louis slammed the phone down and sat on the edge of the bed. He didn't know anything about doctors and hospitals. Never been sick a day in his life. But he had to suppose they knew what they were doing. His forehead broke out in a clammy sweat.

But, driving to the clinic, he convinced himself there was no way they could blame him for Marie showing some crud in her system.

"She was fine when I left. Awake and sipping some tea." Louis tried to look ashamed at leaving his poor sick wife alone. "I never would have left her if I thought she was in danger."

"I see, Mr. Lender." Dr. Chase tapped a pen against his clipboard. "Your wife is a very sick woman. In fact if I thought she could make the trip, I'd send her over to County Hospital. But under the circumstances, we have to try to get her stronger here. Now, I have a few questions."

"I'll try to help any way I can, Doctor."

"Has she been in contact with any water from the river or a pond or standing water?"

"Not that I know of. She doesn't go outside much except to water the gardens and feed the chickens."

"Have you had any trouble with your plumbing or septic tank?"

"No."

"Well, Mr. Lender, your wife's body is inundated with bacteria and parasites, such as the type found in tainted water. I can see you're not affected, so we must assume it's something only she has been in contact with." Dr. Chase arched his bushy eyebrow and peered down his nose at Louis. "I'm not sure we can save her unless we know what she's ingested."

"You mean she might die?" gasped Louis.

"At this point, I think she has a fighting chance."

"So she might be okay?" Louis patted the little vial in his overall pocket.

"With problems of this nature, we can't be sure. I'm sorry Mr. Lender, but without knowing what she's ingested, it's difficult to be certain of anything"

Clearing his throat, Louis stared at his shoes and said, "I'll try to think of everything she's been into. She means the world to me, that woman. Can I go sit with her while I think?"

"I believe that would be fine. If you think of anything, here's my pager number, or contact the nurse immediately." Handing Louis a card, the doctor motioned for him to leave.

Damned doctors were so snooty, acting like they knew everything. Well, some dumb farmer fooled them once, and he could fool them twice.

Marie didn't look much different than she did that morning. But she sure was hooked up and wired for sound. An N bag dangled from a hook above the bed, dripping clear liquid into a needle poked in her forearm. A tube was taped to her nose hooked up to some machine beeping in the corner. Still she rattled when she breathed and her chest rose only a little.

Louis looked around the room, remembering the nurse saying it was their very best. It was nothing special, just plain white, except for a mirror hung on one wall. A red metal box hung on the wall stood out as the only color in the room. White letters printed across the front of the box said, "Toxic! For disposal ONLY. Place all used syringes here."

After checking to make sure no one was in the hallway, Louis flipped up the hinged lid. Peering into the box, he couldn't help but smile like a kid with a cookie jar. Reaching in, he pulled out a small hypodermic syringe. Taking the vial from his pocket, he pulled up the plunger and filled the syringe with the contents. It looked almost luminescent in the fluorescent lighting. Even without his glasses, Louis could see little critters swimming around in the green fluid.

Waiting, he listened for any sounds outside the door. Sitting next to the bed, he gently picked up Marie's hand. "Goodbye darlin'," he said and pressed the needle to the IV tube. But his eye caught a glint of the mirror. In his head he heard, "This is our very best room." Too late...

The judge said he was more "Pond Scum" than stuff from the water. Louis would have a long time to think about that one.

ALL ALONE*
Claire L. Brown

Slouched on a bar stool
Miles from home,
I ordered a pint,
All alone.

An old wrangler shuffled in,
Said, "I knows you, son,"
Staggered a bit...
I wasn't the one.

Weary from runnin,'
I hunkered down,
Eyes tired and bleary,
Brows in a frown.

The run-down saloon
Was quiet as a tomb.
A pot bellied stove
Gave warmth like a womb.

Snorts and guffaws
Were all I heard;
One fellow burped
Through a grizzled beard.

Not caring for talk,
I thought of the trail,
Having ridden for days,
Hell bent for where?

I snatched all her money.
She's broke and alone
With no forwarding address,
And nowhere to phone.

Her folks called me a loser;
I'd guess they was right.
I hustled and gambled,
Stayin' out most the night.

Runnin' from guilt
Is a losing game.
It grabs up your mind,
And drives ya insane.

Now I'm slouched on a bar stool
Miles from home,
Ordering a pint,
All alone.

*ALL ALONE was published in the SUMMIT COUNTY (COLORADO) INDEPENDENT in Aug.,2003.

BUFFALO GALS

Jeanne Freed

Every year, no matter how hard I try, the holidays are insanity. I am haunted by visions of baking, shopping, wrapping, paying bills, and entertaining extended family. It's known to be an incredibly stressful time, but it gets even worse when compounded with FOOTBALL RESPECT.

I am not a Colorado native (shh), and have never been remotely interested in college or pro football. For the sake of peace, I feign joy over "our" teams swell season (really), but highly object to the team's fanatical manipulation of my wardrobe.

An edict was issued on sports talk radio, (another obsession) forbidding anyone to wear red for a month prior to the University of Colorado vs the University of Nebraska game. In case you live in another state, Red is synonymous with Nebraska. Normally this isn't a problem, but when attending Christmas festivities, outlawing the color red makes it difficult to create a holiday ensemble. Besides, I have a red dress I adore, because it hides all of the right things and accents all of the okay things.

But could I wear it to a winter wedding? Only if I wanted to offend the football gods! Instead, Mr. Football's (my husband) protocol insisted I borrow his mother's black and gold suit (apparently she had already learned her lesson). I felt somewhat hostile, but again, for the sake of peace, I wore the stupid suit. CU won, and it was most certainly because of the "MoJo" enhanced by huge retro shoulderpads and linebacker silhouette that insured victory. .

My next faux pas came all too quickly, when I elegantly swept into the room wearing black slacks and a silver threaded sweater. It was after all, the Saturday night before the Broncos vs Raiders game. But I held my own. Did I acquiesce and wear orange? NEVER!

I wore blue.

WISH UPON ...WHAT?

Claire L. Brown

Late, after most had fallen asleep,
I strolled outdoors one mellow night.
Although darkness had descended
The moon switched on a welcome light.

I happened to wish upon a star,
Mere trivial wishes, rather inane,
When suddenly I had to laugh;
My star turned out to be a plane.

I had never wished upon a plane:
"Airplane light, airplane bright,
Grant the wish I wish tonight."
Somehow my ritual became mundane.

I could try a wish, a hope, or prayer,
Allowing ample room to err.
"I wish I may; I wish I might
Wish upon a satellite."

THE RIGHT CHOICE?

Shirley Meier

Janice Fuller settled herself in the empty chair and placed her grade book on her lap, remaining rigid for a second as if she were posing for a picture. She glanced at the well dressed man with big shoulders and touches of grey in his hair who was seated across the room. Next to him was her student, Suzy Clark, who was obviously his daughter. A couple of chairs over, the police consultant of the school sat while the Dean sat facing them from behind his desk.

"Now we are here to talk about Suzy's referral of insubordination from Miss Fuller's English class," the Dean said, his eyes moving in a slow deliberate survey of everyone in the room. Of course, they all knew why they had gathered and Janice knew the more serious charge of drug possession would be dealt with later by the authorities.

He continued. "Suzy, can you tell us your perception of the incident?" Administrators always used that technique for fairness, but Janice also knew it to be a device to cover their backs.

Suzy, a girl of fifteen with long curly brown hair, pursed her lips and said nothing. She was a very attractive girl, thought Janice, but with one obvious flaw. She couldn't remember her ever smiling, as if something hard held her lips in place. That hardness showed now as they all waited for her response. Janice felt that having disruption in a classroom was one thing, but replaying it seldom conveyed the true situation. It either increased the tension or, conversely, failed to fully capture the dynamics of the situation.

"Tell us what happened, Suzy. This is your chance to speak," said her father in a resonant but intense voice. She, however, sat unmoved and stared at the wall. Janice recognized the behavior as a planned strategy not to give anything away. Many times, remedial students were ready with noisy and uncontrolled defenses but Suzy wasn't one to easily let go. That's why her cursing fray in class was unusual and her anger, as she threw a magazine at the teacher, was a total surprise. But the greatest shock had been when a pouch of coke, obviously put in the magazine, had neatly dropped out on the desk.

Mr. Clark shifted his weight and glanced uncomfortably at the Dean's desk where Suzy's discipline folder lay opened. For a student who had just transferred from Florida last year, it hadn't taken her much time at Hawkins High to provide enough referrals for a thick paper file.

They waited. The clock ticked and Janice tapped her toe. She knew the girl had a problem beyond the classroom and it made her wish she could help. But this meeting was taking away from her planning period and that bothered her. She was dedicated to teaching and felt she did a good job, but right now, the setting made her wish she were somewhere else. Perhaps on a beach in Bermuda, or a dim room filed with soft music. She guessed the others in the room might also be feeling uncomfortable.

Suddenly Suzy said, "OK I had some dope. Big deal. And I probably spouted off to her. So if you got to bust me, go ahead. I just want to get out of here."

"Tell us more about what was happening before the incident," continued the Dean, almost avoiding the confession of possession. He was trying hard to define his teacher's interaction with the student.

"She was hassling me. I couldn't stand it."

"What exactly were you doing?"

Janice hated these question and answer dramas. The father, looking toward her for the first time, seemed to be appraising her expression but she maintained her crisp teacher look, mastered in twelve years of teaching.

"We had to read, read, and I hate to read," said Suzy. "You know, every day, so boring. Besides 1 know how to read. So I told her so."

"Would you call your behavior disruptive, insubordinate?" said the Dean, but continued without waiting for the answer. He went for the jugular. "Did you throw the magazine at your teacher and call her a bitch?"

"Ya, if she says so," said the girl flippantly, glancing at the discipline folder.

"Anything you want to add, Miss Fuller, in addition to your referral here?"

"No, I don't think so."

"Now let's deal with the other issues. Mr. Clark, according to the nurse's report, Suzy was also under chemical influence during this incident."

Janice relaxed in her chair, her contribution over, but she couldn't help but be slightly aggravated at the language, calling everything an incident. In the classroom the obvious disrespect was often a call to war, a battle of wills, not an incident.

"Suzy, for insubordination, repeated discipline problems, " said the Dean, glancing again at the folder, "you are suspended for two weeks and are required to attend our chemical abuse seminar before returning. The police consultant will handle the possession charge later in his office."

Janice started to get up, assuming the conference was over, but Mr. Clark's painful voice stopped her.

"I don't think a seminar session will be enough," he said. "I can see there's a bigger problem here to solve. I'm going to have Suzy undergo rehabilitation. There's a unit at City Central Hospital, I believe. I understand she can continue with her studies, by tutoring or alternate education there."

"What do you mean, Dad?" The girl jumped up, alarmed. "We didn't talk about that. What are you doing?"

"We talked about getting along at school, not getting into drugs."

Janice nervously fingered her papers because it was one of those horrible moments when peoples' lives lay open, like pages of a book. Glancing at Suzy's face, she didn't see the defiance or the challenging contempt that was so much of her character. She saw the girl gaze dumbfounded at her father and it was obvious that he meant a great deal to her.

"There's no other way," he said quietly and rose. "Thank you all for your time." He nodded and touched Suzy's arm as they left.

The Dean heaved a sigh and Janice moved to leave. She was glad it was over. Of course, she didn't feel guilty. Any responsible teacher couldn't let a thing like that pass, even if it were difficult. But part of her always wished that she could do more to solve her students' problems. She longed for the days when the drug problem hadn't been so prevalent and she could teach bright, unmotivated kids like Suzy with gentle learning. Now most of them were too strung out or angry to notice her efforts. The dealers who got kids into this mess affected her life too and she hated them for it. She knew she failed far too often but that was the reality of the job.

A few days later as she passed the main office, she heard a man's voice behind her. " Oh, Miss Fuller, I'm so glad to catch you. I wonder if you have a minute?"

She turned and saw Suzy's father. Immediately she felt tense. Now what? He was dressed in a smart blue suit and he seemed much taller than she remembered. His eyes looked straight at her, entirely in command.

"I've picked up some of Suzy's work. I want to thank you for getting together these lesson outlines so quickly. The tutors at rehab will appreciate that, I'm sure."

"We're required to do that," she said coolly. It was one of her favorite aggravations. Enough to teach kids in the classroom but to provide extra materials for outside students really stretched her patience.

119

I'd like to talk with you about her English studies. It doesn't seem to be her favorite class and I know it's important."

Janice smiled. Nice way to put it, she thought ruefully, but she noted his earnest tone and said, "I'm glad to help. Let's go to the lounge where we can talk and have a cup of coffee."

So that was how they met and kept on meeting. First meeting for a drink and talking about Suzy but after a while they talked about work and went to the movies. When they started going into the city for the evening, they talked about life and each other. Paul Clark was in real estate and had lost his wife in a car accident several years ago. She told him about her schooling and her interesting studies abroad, eliminating her rather sterile childhood. When she invited him for dinner at her apartment, they talked about love and he stayed long into the night.

Later, they took a trip together to Florida during Spring break as Paul had some business with a condominium complex there and Janice relished a change of pace. They spent time on the protected beach behind the club house where the fuzziness of the distant lake shoreline cut the world into two blue categories one moist and soothing, the other cool and ethereal.

It was a setting for desire as he ran his hand slowly over her hips. She squirmed because she was ticklish but she loved it. The world seemed perfect.

"You won't mind if I take off this afternoon for a bit, will you? I've got to meet some fellows I used to know when I lived here. They've got some strips on a couple of lakes just north of here. Worth developing."

She did mind but understood. She admired his tanned body as he walked back to the unit and then she rolled over, stretching long and digging into the sand with her toes at the edge of the towel. It felt good to be in love with Paul Clark. He had proved witty and fun loving, quite overshadowing some of the sadness in his life. He was well traveled and sophisticated, which appealed to her standards. And he had money, it seemed lots of it.

Paul found her again on the beach when he returned. "Let's go out in the sailboat!" he said and they raced off to the pier. She could tell he was especially happy as they tacked noiselessly to the opposite point on the lake.

"Please, drop the sail. I just want to stay here forever. This is our special place, " she said.

"Just what I was thinking."

They stretched out and pressed close to one another on the deck. "Be careful, or we'll roll right off."

How good she felt and glad that she had come, even though there had been a momentary prudish hesitation at his invitation. He'd also constantly surprised her with gifts, sometimes making her feel a little bought and it disturbed her.

"You know, you're not bad for the usual dumpy schoolteacher," he said teasingly.

"You're a pretty hot number for a lonely widower yourself."

They had become comfortable enough with each other to touch on delicate topics. She knew, after all, that she was attractive and experienced as well as being educated, liberated, and professional. Her confidence and moderate ego had sent several men scrambling but she hadn't lost many that she'd cared about. But liking her own terms, Janice Fuller hadn't ever made a real commitment either. However, now she could only think of the man beside her. It was warmly disconcerting. The real thing? It seemed so right.

"Jan?"

"Yes," she said, thinking how appealing and sensitive he was.

"Janice Fuller," he said seriously, touching her hand and staring up into the sky. "Will you marry me?"

"Oh, Paul, " she said. She should be taken aback but actually she felt it was totally normal. Rolling over on the hot boat deck, she saw his face forcibly controlled, much as she had seen him that day in the conference. It was the look of something important.

"You are the most beautiful thing I've even had in my life. I love you and we both need you. Say yes."

Their faces were an inch apart. It was quiet for a long moment and then a speeding motor boat came around the point and whizzed past them, sending sharp waves in its wake. Their boat bounced up and down, making them almost slide off the deck. He grabbed her with one hand and with the other steadied himself with the mast.

"That was a surprise," said Janice.

"What was? The boat or the proposal?"

"Both."

"So?"

"Let me think about it, Paul."

"Not if you ever want to get off this boat," he said and his voice and face lost their seriousness. He laughed. "You do want to get off this boat eventually, right?"

"Yes, I do."

"Ah, ha. I knew it. The lady said yes. She said it," he said, jumping up and nearly tipping the boat.

It was raining and cool. Janice settled in front of the fire that Paul had made in his living room. How she looked forward to these evenings. She closed her eyes and tried to dismiss all the classroom routine out of her mind. They had just finished dinner and were having an after dinner drink. He came into the room, carrying a bottle and glasses in his hand and bent to kiss her.

"What are you thinking about, Jan?"

"Oh. Just classroom stuff. Also, about Suzy. You should tell her about us. It's only right."

"I already have, you know that."

"But not who I am. Janice as in Fuller. Miss Fuller. That's a big part of it."

She could see him becoming tense. His last few visits to the rehab, she knew, had been difficult.

"It wasn't time. Couldn't jeopardize her emotional state with too many outside details. But she is getting strong. In fact, she is probably coming home tomorrow and I'll tell her then."

"Tomorrow? Really, Paul?"

"They called me yesterday."

"You just said the other day you still had misgivings."

"True, but it seems they think she's ready. I hope I am."

The door bell rang and he kissed her again lightly. She thought she had never seen him so handsome with ruffled hair and open collar. And he was a good man, so dedicated to the well being of his daughter. She sank back on the pillow and kicked off her shoes, getting herself comfortable as Paul went toward the entry. He made a referee's time out signal with his hands and she smiled back at him. The bell rang again, it seemed rather insistently, but he kept looking at her.

"Oh, go, get the door."

"O.K., O.K. But don't go away, as they say in the movies."

She heard the door open and a throaty voice say, "Hi, Dad!"

"Suzy! You're here. I mean...now? I didn't..."

"So, you didn't expect me."

Janice quickly retrieved her shoes as she heard the luggage in the hall being moved.

"I thought I'd give you a surprise. Actually I left but you can sign me out tomorrow," Suzy said as she entered the living room. Her hair was cut shorter and she seemed thin. She spotted Janice and stopped. A long moment followed.

"Miss Fuller?" she said with hesitation.

Janice didn't know what to say. She was as shocked as Suzy, so she mumbled, "Nice for you to be home, Suzy."

Suzy just stared at her. "Miss Fuller?" Wheels were turning in her head.

Paul interrupted. "Suzy, this is Janice. You remember her as Miss Fuller." Janice could hear a helpless quality in his voice that she'd never sensed before, and it added to the discomfort of the moment.

"I know who she is, Dad, but what in the world is she doing here?"

"Sit down, Suzy;" he said, assuming more control. "I know this is tough and it isn't the way I wanted it to happen, believe me. I didn't know you were coming tonight. Are you sure that it's all right? I need to sign you out."

Janice's stomach felt like a rock and she couldn't breathe. Nothing about the room or Paul or her world was the same as a minute ago. She felt every muscle snap against the heaviness that was pushing down on her.

"Perhaps, I'll go clean up the kitchen and you two can talk," she said quickly, excusing herself.

She closed the door and braced herself against the counter. She didn't want to hear them in the other room so she began to rinse the strewn dishes and stacked them into the dishwasher. It was full and she turned it on but it had a very quiet hum and the sound didn't fill the empty place. She saw that the other dirty kettles were on the stove so she gathered them up, ran the water and scrubbed them clean. She tried to make as much noise as possible but the voices in the other room still were audible.

"She's wonderful, give her a chance, Suzy. You could have a mother again."

"I don't need a mother right now, Dad. You're more than I can handle."

Janice turned on the radio to drown out the voices. Frantically she rummaged through the drawer looking for more scrub pads or cleaning supplies. She was almost willing to scrub the floor. In one cupboard she found an immense supply of small plastic bags.

"Oh, I love him, love him. But there's Suzy. This is such a mess," she moaned to herself as she dunked the pans again furiously under the water. She started to cry and her tears fell into the soapy water, making little rings. "I was kidding myself. I knew she'd hate me and I really don't like her much either. But I'd like her for his sake. I'd do anything for him."

She wiped her hands and face. The music on the radio was ironically romantic but it didn't drown out the loud voices from the other room.

"I did it because I loved you." Paul was explaining.

"You did it because I was a lot of trouble, " Suzy said, the earlier surprised anguish replaced by colder fury. "Don't you know that I finally figured you out? I know what you're into, Dad. Believe me, I had enough time in there to put it together."

Janice couldn't help herself. She had to hear more and she moved to the door. Obviously, his daughter had come home with more resentment than when she had left. "I love him. How can I help him?" she said softly.

"You've got to understand," said Paul in a subdued voice from the other room. "It's different now. I'm different now. I changed when you got into dope."

"I bet," said Suzy, laughing. "We were always such buddies, you said. I thought you were so cool. And you're real smooth, that's for sure. Never touched the stuff yourself, did you, except to pass it on? Never thought I'd get into it too. Not so cool. This is actually all your fault, don't you see?"

"When I saw what drugs did to you, I died. It's true. My own kid. Then I met Janice and..."

"Does she know the score? How about those trips to Florida? Meeting the guys on the lake, picking up the drop offs?"

"I got out of that this spring. No more Florida connection."

Janice grabbed the door knob. It balanced her and she hung on to it. She didn't believe what she was hearing.

"You've got to be kidding, Dad! A supplier doesn't stop. They're more addicted to their habits than we users are. They like the money, they don't care about anything else."

"But, Suzy, I have..."

"Besides if she finds out, she'll be history anyway, let me tell you. She's one square lady so we don't have to worry about her being around."

"Janice won't..."

"Hey, get real. Even if 1 don't like her, she's the only honest one here and you know it. She won't buy it."

Janice flung open the door and saw Paul and Suzy glaring at one another. She could only whisper, "Paul, what's happening?"

"Scratch me out then, Suzy," he said slowly as he pulled Janice to his side. "But give her a chance, please."

"Tell her, Dad. Tell the school teacher."

A long quiet pause followed.

"The school teacher heard," said Janice painfully.

Then Paul said, "Suzy, we're too upset. We can't discuss this any more right now. I have to check rehab and see what they say. We need some time."

"We'll need more than that," said Suzy, grabbing her suitcases and stomping out of the room.

"Paul, I think I need to go home," Janice said, almost numb.

" I don't understand, don't know how to understand what I heard."

"What you heard? I know it sounds bad but I can explain." Paul's voice elevated and he coughed. "I'll help you understand. It's going to be all right, my darling. Everything is different now. All because of you. I'm OK now, don't you see?"

"OK? OK with what? We'll have to talk later," she said, reaching for her coat in the closet. Glancing at the empty doorway, she added, "All I know now is that Suzy needs you. You have to straighten that out. And I certainly complicate your life with her." She ached with the thought of how complicated her own life had just become. Her head ached and her heart thumped.

"Janice, please..."

"And what she says about you, I can't..."

"Don't believe it, don't. My past life is over. It's different now."

"Different? Different from what?"

"You've changed my life, Janice. You could change hers too. Don't you see that I love you so much?"

Paul's face was red and he stepped forward, grabbing her arms. He was the man she loved but she didn't know if she recognized him. In addition to her shock, she suddenly felt a faint hint of fear by his movement.

"I can explain everything." he pleaded, releasing her.

"I can't listen to your explanation right now, Paul." She looked into his eyes, softening at his despair. She wanted to believe him so much, but could she? Her foggy indecision said, "I might call you in a few days."

"Good, then we'll talk. I know we need some time but you'll understand, Jan. I know you will. I know you'll do the right thing."

"The right thing? What's the right choice here?" She rolled her eyes toward the stairs and then dropped her eyes, digging for the keys in her pocket.

WHY GRAFFITI?*
Claire L. Brown

A frustrated vandal's urge for power,
Wildly scribbling without getting caught.

An unhappy vandal's urge to destroy,
Made happier, strangely, while destroying.

An angry vandal's urge to produce ugliness
For surroundings to match a troubled state of mind.

A bored vandal's urge to express freedom of speech
With no accompanying responsibility.

A belligerent vandal's urge to stake out territory
Like a cat defecating in a garden.

*WHY GRAFFITI was published in the SUMMIT COUNTY (COLORADO) INDEPENDENT, Aug.,2003.

WHOA!

CLOUD

A puff, airy, full
White, then trimmed pink, to crimson
–Birth, life, perfect end.

-Shirley Meier

TRAGEDY
(9/11/01)
Claire L. Brown

Glass shattering
Walls crumbling;
The world as we know it,
Ending

Stars and stripes rising
Amidst rubble smoking. .
Firemen bleary eyed,
Singing

Refrains resounding
Of God Bless America.
Citizens rallying,
Valiantly.

CATHY'S LOBSTER DINNER*
Jeanne Freed

Cathy looked at the object in her hand and puzzled over its possible use. It was shiny and silvery... an unusual shape. Actually, it was quite pretty. Perhaps she could wear it in her hair. "Cathy? Are you okay?"

Dragging her eyes from they shiny object, she looked into the concerned eyes of the man who was always there. Such a handsome man. She smiled. "I'm fine."

"Then put down the fork, and let's clean up the dishes."

"Dishes? Yes, let's clean the dishes." "Are you sure you're okay?"

"It's time." "No, it's too soon."

"It's the right time, Tom. I feel it slipping away. You promised."

"Have you decided which restaurant?"

"I wrote it down a long time ago. It's all in the memory book. You know where it is."

"Did you write down who you wanted to come?"

"Yes. Let's remember to invite Aunt Esther. She needs a night out."

"Esther died three years ago, Cathy."

"Oh yes, I must have forgotten."

"I'll call for reservations. Would three weeks from Saturday be okay?"

"Is that a long time?" "No. It's a very short time, depending on how you look at it."

"Does it give everyone enough time to get here. The girls will need sitters for the babies, you know."

"I'm sure it will work out fine."

"I think I'll take a nap."

"That's a good idea, you look tired. You rest, I'll take care of the arrangements."

Cathy sat straight and prim, just as mother taught her. It would never do for a young lady to sit slouched like an old pillow. After all, this was her perfect party. Everyone was coming. Tom said so. They would never miss a party for Cathy. She loved them all so very much. They loved her too. The idea of a spring party seemed quite welcome. "Cathy Barkin requests the honor of your presence at SEAFOOD LANDING, 7:00 pin Saturday the tenth of May." Something different, they all said. No one asked why.

"Mom, you look beautiful." "Thank you, Ellen."

"I'm Sharon, Mom."

130

"I'm sorry, you looked like Ellen in this light. Doesn't this room look beautiful? This is such a nice restaurant."

"Yes, it is beautiful. I don't remember you ever talking about it, why did you pick this place"

"Lobster sounded so good to me. I've had a taste for it lately."

"Oh look, there's Cousin Betty. My goodness it's like a family reunion. I haven't seen some of these people in years."

"We wanted everyone here, dear. We thought it would be nice to see everyone together again."

People in all shapes and sizes hugged Cathy and told her how pretty she looked. Was that her brother Sam? Oh well, it didn't matter.

A toast? A handsome young man called her Grandma. Everyone clapped She felt like a princess.

Cathy sat at the end of along table. The lobster rested on a pretty blue plate next to a wedge of lemon. It was just a tail, but it looked meaty. Cathy cut a piece and dipped it into a small brazier of melted butter. She paused for just an instant. The man she'd known for so long was watching her. She smiled at him and mouthed the warm words; "I love you".

Tom touched her hand and whispered, "Always, Cathy, always."

It was so sweet and moist. The lobster was everything she hoped for. It was perfect. She'd never been so happy.

The notice in the paper was exactly as Cathy wished:

CATHY BARKIN, age 79, passed away at St. Elizabeth's Hospital, May 11, 2000. Severe allergic reaction to shellfish led to respiratory arrest. In lieu of flowers, the family requests contributions to the Alzheimer's Association.

CATHY'S LOBSTER DINNER first appeared in SKUNK'S TALES 1996

Author's Note: There is a new reformation in the air begun by everyday believers who have grown weary of absolute directives, strict non Biblical dogma, and recitations within the framework of bureaucratic hierarchy, both ancient and modern. Consequently, I have written a New Millennium Creed:

NEW MILLENNIUM CREED
Claire L. Brown

I believe in one eternal and all powerful God, creator of the universe.

I believe in God's only son, Jesus, who became the Christ, who was born of his beloved mother, Mary, was betrayed by Judas, suffered under the Roman ruler, Pontius Pilate, was crucified, died, and was buried.

On the third day He rose from the dead, and dwelt among believers, just as His Spirit does today.

I believe in the community of Christians, known as the Church, and in its potential to express and share the word of God, as recorded in the Bible.

I believe in the teachings of Jesus, the Golden Rule, the power of prayer, and the forgiveness of sin.

I believe that God is Wisdom, Truth, and Love.

Amen

SOUNDS OF SORROW
Jeanne Freed

Ask anybody, "What sound do you like?" and "What sound do you hate?" Almost everyone has a unique and individual answer. We love the noise of laughter, bells caroling, the babble of a mountain stream, and hate jackhammers, sirens, and snores. The gurgle of a baby's laughter from a game of peek a boo, or the constant yip of a poodle begging to be let in the house, makes up the sounds of life. Pleasing euphony or raucous discord stirs memories and can create pleasure or make us cry.

In the past I rather enjoyed hearing helicopters fly over, imagining a heroic rescue or a high speed chase through town. But on April 20, 1999, I learned to hate the sound of helicopters. While Eric Harris and Dylan Klebold performed their unthinkable massacre at Columbine High School in Littleton, Colorado my home was directly below the "safe zone" or the legally determined mile away from the crime scene. As we slowly realized the horror unfolding so close to our home and family, we could not escape the media's new form of torment. Helicopters hovered over our roof or back yard for three days, the rotors cacophony constant, strident, and disturbing. Never again will I hear the sound without remembering those heartrending and poignant days. But perhaps because I am so keenly tuned to the sound of helicopters, I will remember because of the noise, and always think of the lives lost. If never forgetting is a true commitment, then a sound from above is all I need to remember.

On September 11, 2001, after terrorists attacked and crumbled the World Trade Centers, sound was hushed. For days, the subliminal roar of jets thirty thousand feet above, halted and it was the loudest silence I ever heard. The echo of a military jet became a fascination. A hush so prevailing that it became palpable. A quiet so obvious and peculiar that I realized I never "heard" stillness before. Later, the reverberation of a 747's engines became a dulcet melody causing me to stop and listen.

Two of the most horrific occurrences of my lifetime were marked by a deafening roar and an absolute quiet. . . the sounds of sorrow.

TEN (plus 3) PERSONAL COMMANDMENTS
(Hints for Living)
Claire L. Brown

Love and revere the one true God.

Treat others as you wish to be treated, never hurting another verbally or physically.

Love and respect yourself and others; we all are equal in the eyes of God.

Be more than fair or just, adding a dash of kindness.

Forgive, and forgive. and forgive again.

Be truthful and honest in everything , without anticipation of reward.

Keep vows and promises.

Believe in the power of daily prayer.

Work toward peace with love and diligence.

When in charge, retain humility, remembering that you are a servant of your people.

Retain a youthful sense of wonder and awe.

Acknowledge the fact that you are loved by God (no matter what...), abandoning feelings of guilt.

Remember that life is a gift from God. Use it well.

As you keep these commandments, may you become closer to God, Wisdom, and Truth, and live a fuller, more balanced and abundant life.

OFF WHITE

Jeanne Freed

Most standard application forms have little boxes to check requesting ethnic background information. One box says Caucasian, and though I've always checked that box, I'm not certain I should. The dictionary says "Caucasian" means the people of Caucasus. Though I have a general idea where Caucasus is, I have never heard any of the elders in my family mention it as homeland.

Webster's "New World Dictionary" defines the word **Caucasoid**:
(adj) "[[from the erroneous notion that the original home of the hypothetical Indo-Europeans was Caucasus]] designating or of one of the major geographical varieties of human being, including peoples of Europe, Africa, the Near East, India, etc.: who are generally characterized by tall stature, straight or wavy hair, etc.: loosely called the *white race* although it embraces many peoples of dark skin color."

Starting with "*the erroneous notion*", and then moving on to the "*hypothetical Indo-Europeans*", and finally "*embraces many peoples of dark skin color*", doesn't exactly convince me that "Caucasian" is the appropriate box for . . .uh . . . well . . .uh . . . persons like me.

My paternal grandfather was Dutch, and my paternal grandmother was Welsh. On the maternal side, I have an Irish grandmother and a German grandfather. So each of my parents was half-something, and that makes me one quarter of four different countries of origin, or a Euro-Quad-American (EQA). Keeping this equation, and proceeding to the next generation and assuming that my children, who by now are Euro-Octa Americans (EOA), blend and homogenize, this entire concept becomes unwieldy and nearly unfathomable.

This was proven before by the Civil War era southern states penchant for calling slaves Mulatto when one parent was black, and the other white. They took it a step further and deemed a person Quadroon if they were the child of a Mulatto and a white or Octoroon if the child of a Quadroon and a white. Since it must have been difficult to keep track of the exact mix, the terms became antiquated. Then the people of dark toned skin became known as Negros or Colored People for a while, then Blacks, and more recently, either African Americans or People of Color.

135

Native American Indians were dubbed "Redskins", while Orientals were called Yellow-skinned. So we have altered our thinking and given the "Reds" the nobility of calling themselves "Native Americans", and the "Yellows" became Asian Americans, the "Blacks" are African Americans, and yet I am still just a Caucasian or "White".

In a country priding itself on freedom and diversity, I must question why the term "White" hasn't been eliminated in favor of a more correct category. Perhaps a more descriptive word, like Ivory, Cream, Snow, Bisque, Linen, Alabaster, Ecru, Putty, Oyster, or Eggshell could be supplied. After all, those are names used for paint. White isn't good enough to paint the living-room, so why is it good enough when choosing my skin color.

True, in the winter I do call my flesh "pasty", but even then it has miniscule red bumps, and some freckles, and is overall more of a pale peach with hints of beige. In the summer, I can either be red, pink, bronzed tan, spotted, and once again partially pasty. But, unless I've been soaking too long in a tub of hot water, I am not white.

Ethnic groups have been broken down into Asian Americans, Italian Americans, Irish Americans, African Americans, Native Americans, Mexican Americans, German Americans and countless other identities. How many Americans can claim with certainty, they are purebred for multiple generations? For those of us who are homogenized with blended gene pools, we've got nothing to call ourselves. Some people say "Heinz 57", which is also the term used for a mixed breed mutt, or ketchup.

Every other color requests respect and to be called by some subjective, politically correct designation. Well, I too am proud of my ancestors, and the struggles they endured for our freedoms. Why can't every cultural gene pool be allowed equal silliness? I don't want to be called "White" anymore. I'm an Integrated European American (IEA). Or more specifically, an Integrated Northern European American (INEA). I want equality, fair treatment, and a little race/origin box on every form where I can freely and honestly make my checkmark.

Not White. Not Caucasian. But I might settle for a dignified "Cream" or "Bisque".

THE INFLUENCE (OR NOT) OF BOOKS
Claire L. Brown

Notice whenever renowned authors are asked,
"What did you read in your youth?"
They consistently cite a grandiose work,
Never something trite or uncouth.

Whatever type story inspired my reading,
Of danger, adventure or flight;
It kept me poring through pages,
Filling me with delight.

My initial interest was piqued,
Not by the literarily great and good,
But by stories catching my fancy,
Those which I well understood.

Reading, as with other habits
Can become a type of addiction.
Whenever I can I hunker down
To indulge my bookish affliction

There are no pills to cure me,
Or rituals with which to atone.
Just let me select a book or two,
Then allow me time alone.

By the way...
I'm in a hurry to leave now.
A good book awaits me at home,
And if I don't soon bid adieu'
I may never end this poem.

CLAIRE LERAAN BROWN

Claire Leraan Brown grew up in Duluth, Minnesota. She graduated from the University of Colorado with a degree in Psychology. For several years she and her husband, Tom, enjoyed a second home in Brighton, England, where family and friends often visited. Presently she is an active community volunteer, participates in the Great Books program, spends time at the family mountain cabin in Frisco, Colorado, travels extensively, and relaxes in her canoe and on the tennis court.

JEANNE FREED

Though born in Illinois, Jeanne Freed has called Colorado home for twenty years. She was also fortunate enough to spend many wonderful years in New Mexico, resulting in a great love of the southwest and its unique culture. Always a ravenous reader, she began writing after a debilitating illness and the realization that life is too short. She is the mother of two college aged daughters, and two un-educated golden retrievers. When not writing, she wears many hats: spending time running a small xeric (drought tolerant) gardening business, volunteering, enjoying friends, crafting, crocheting and looking forward to traveling more with her husband, Tim.

SHIRLEY MEIER

Shirley Ding Meier, a native of North Dakota, worked in professional theater before a career teaching English in Chicago's suburban high schools. A graduate of the University of Montana with her Master's from Northern Illinois University, she also studied in Mexico City and London. During that time she published articles and spoke at national and international conventions about education. Now retired to Colorado, she and her husband Henry have two daughters, three grandchildren and share an interest in travel, fine arts and gardening.

ORDER FORM

Please send _____ copies of *VIEWS FROM JACKASS HILL* @ $12.00 /copy + $2.00 Shipping and Handling (Add $1 for each additional copy ordered) + 3% tax (for CO residents only) for each copy. I have enclosed a check or money order, made payable to Jeanne Freed for $ _____

Mail to: Jeanne Freed
5141 West Fremont Drive
Littleton, CO 80123
Phone (303) 972 2565

Name	
Address	
City	State/Province
Zip/Postal Code	Phone
E-mail (optional)	

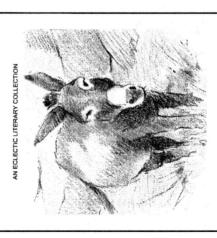

VIEWS... *From JACKASS HILL*

AN ECLECTIC LITERARY COLLECTION

CLAIRE LERAAN BROWN,
JEANNE FREED, SHIRLEY MEIER

Printed in the United States
54278LVS00002B/1-201

9 781932 852578